M000284659

Women Remembered

Women Remembered

Jesus' Female Disciples

HELEN BOND and JOAN TAYLOR

HODDER &
STOUGHTON

First published in Great Britain in 2022 by Hodder & Stoughton
An Hachette UK company

I

Copyright © Helen Bond and Joan Taylor, 2022

The right of Helen Bond and Joan Taylor to be identified as the
Author of the Work has been asserted by them in accordance
with the Copyright, Designs and Patents Act 1988.

A CIP catalogue record for this title is available from the British Library

Hardback ISBN 978 1 529 37259 5
eBook ISBN 978 1 529 37261 8

Typeset in Bembo MT by Hewer Text UK Ltd, Edinburgh
Printed and bound in Great Britain by Clays Ltd, Elcograf S.p.A.

Hodder & Stoughton policy is to use papers that are natural, renewable
and recyclable products and made from wood grown in sustainable
forests. The logging and manufacturing processes are expected to
conform to the environmental regulations of the country of origin.

Hodder & Stoughton Ltd
Carmelite House
50 Victoria Embankment
London EC4Y 0DZ

www.hodderfaith.com

In celebration of car chat,
and with thanks to Anna and JC

Contents

Prologue

About the Authors, and a Documentary

This book is authored by two professors of Christian Origins who share a common passion to reach beyond the ivory towers of university education and to share their knowledge and research with a wider audience. Our long years of research and many publications have led us to high positions within our fields, but often what we say is not widely heard outside the limited circles of conferences and seminars. We both enjoy giving public talks and writing for wider audiences, and love opportunities to share ideas on television or radio.

A few years ago, we pitched a television programme to Jean-Claude Bragard of Minerva Media, who successfully got it commissioned by Channel 4's Secret History series. *Jesus' Female Disciples: The New Evidence* (Minerva Pictures for Channel 4, 2018) is a documentary that marries old and new material, our

Joan and Helen: intrepid researchers of Jesus' Female Disciples *(2018)*

own research and that of others, as we search to illuminate the women who were part of Jesus' mission and their legacy. Directed by the gifted Anna Cox, the programme attracted a UK audience of 1.4 million (subsequently shown in Europe, Australia, New Zealand, Scandinavia and elsewhere in the world) and received more press coverage than any other religious programme since the BBC's *Son of God* in 2001. It featured in the *Independent*, *The Times*, and the *Guardian*. Six national newspapers cited it as 'Pick of the Day'. *The Sunday Times* named it 'Critics' Choice', and declared, 'It is worth hoping that this engaging and intrepid presenting duo are given more films to present together.'* *Black Christian News*, *Christianity Today*, *Church News* and the international Catholic magazine the *Tablet* aided uptake among Christians on both sides of the Atlantic.

This documentary lies behind the present book. During our travels we filmed in Jordan, Israel and Italy with a small team of two cameramen, a sound recordist and the director, helped by fixers along the way. As we moved from one location to another, we met many experts and ended up with far too much material for a fifty-minute film. We constantly debated between ourselves, chatting as we drove in the hired car, imagining the lives of the women who travelled with Jesus, using all our skills and expertise to think afresh. Even the precise wording of the biblical texts was challenged, as we made our own versions of the original Greek (many of which are in the present book).

We first scribbled down the notes for this book while waiting for hours in the crowded transit hall of the Allenby Bridge crossing, going from Jordan to Israel over the Jordan River, with a firm sense that we ourselves were learning more than we had anticipated. Even being on the road opened our eyes to new things. Journeying with a mission now is very different from two thousand years ago, but, in the intensity and troubles of travels, in the camaraderie and crises, standing in the locations where those early spreaders of Jesus' message stood, we got some clearer glimpses of what it was like for Jesus' first female disciples.

*Victoria Segal in the *The Sunday Times*, 8 April 2018.

The film crew — Minerva Media — in the field

During our talks to various groups after the documentary, and in a huge number of emails, many people have asked us if there's a book they could have that shares what we talked about on film. This is it, with extras.

We hope you enjoy travelling with us again, as we open the door to you to join us.

Helen Bond and Joan Taylor, August 2021

Introduction

Where Are the Women?

Did Jesus have female disciples? Popular memory would say no. The whole Christian tradition of sermons, art, film and theatre remembers Jesus as surrounded by twelve male disciples, his constant companions and confidants. Images of Jesus surrounded by a group consisting only of men are among the most famous works of art in the world: think of Leonardo da Vinci's iconic painting *The Last Supper* (1495–6). Jesus sits in the middle of a long table, with six men to his right and six men to his left, and whoever served the food has clearly departed.

Not only are women not imagined as being part of Jesus' mission, but the story of Christianity's spread is also a masculine one. In the first century – so the story goes – the Christian

Leonardo da Vinci, The Last Supper *(1495-7)*

I

message was taken to the lands around the Mediterranean by two great men: Peter and Paul. And later on, the message was reflected upon and transposed into creedal statements in the third and fourth centuries by the 'Fathers' of the Church. In popular memory, then, the history of earliest Christianity is decidedly male.

But is this the full story? One piece of evidence suggests it's not. Sometime in the late 50 CE, Paul wrote a letter to the church in Rome. This was one of the most important letters that Paul would ever write, setting out his beliefs and hoping that the church would welcome him when he came to visit. As he was still something of an unknown quantity among the Roman Christians, he finished his letter with a list of important people he knew there. Many of them worked with him. What's fascinating about this list is that it's the closest we have to a snapshot of the early church, a random collection of people who are listed simply because they were known to Paul. And the surprising thing is that, of the twenty-nine names in the chapter, eleven – more than one-third of them – are women. These women were clearly performing various roles in the church – deacons, benefactors/ leaders or 'apostles' (envoys) – and others were running house churches.

Romans 16

Most significant of all is the fact that the letter itself was delivered by a woman, Phoebe (Paul wrote to *commend* her to people who didn't already know her, strongly implying that she had been sent from him with the letter). It's very unlikely that Phoebe was just the postwoman; as a 'deacon' (minister) and benefactor/leader in her own right, she presumably read out and defended Paul's lengthy missive. She was not just Paul's deputy, but also an able teacher, envoy and negotiator.

So how do we explain the presence of so many women in the Christian movement in the 50s when they seem to have been absent earlier, in Jesus' mission?

If we look carefully at the Gospels we'll see that there is more evidence for women in the mission of Jesus than we first supposed. Here and there women do appear. They aren't always named, and sometimes their stories are tantalisingly brief, but traces of Jesus' women disciples haven't been completely rubbed away. And this is significant. In a patriarchal and hierarchical society where ordinary women's involvement in anything was commonly overlooked or erased, the very fact that *any* women are mentioned at all is worthy of note.

The Gospel writers weren't interested in telling us about female disciples – they wrote to tell us about Jesus, to inspire faith in him and (in the case of the Acts of the Apostles) to tell us how great missionaries took the message to Rome. Where women are mentioned, it's usually a passing reference or the tiniest of clues. But these traces repay careful investigation, and we're justified in assuming that far more lies behind these clues than we might initially suppose – they represent the tip of the iceberg, we might say.

Two examples from the Gospel of Mark provide illustrations of this. In one story in the Gospel (3:20–35), Jesus' family came to take him home. He'd been so busy preaching and healing all day that he hadn't had a chance to eat anything, and people were starting to say he'd gone crazy. As the family stood outside, a message got to Jesus that his mother and siblings had come for him. But Jesus ignored them. What was important to him wasn't heritage but faith. In a fundamental change to how 'family' was defined, Jesus looked at the people gathered around him and said, 'Whoever does the will of God is my brother and sister and mother.'

It's often noted that this passage is hard on Jesus' mother Mary; in Mark's Gospel she's not presented as a believer, and her natural maternal desire to protect her son got in the way of his mission. But more importantly, it's clear that the people gathered around Jesus included women, and Jesus included sisters and mothers in his vision of the new family group that was forming around him. The absence of 'fathers' here, in the deeply patriarchal society of the ancient Mediterranean world, also says something about the way Jesus saw this new community in which sisters and mothers were playing an equal role under the fatherhood of God.

A second example comes right at the very end of Mark's Gospel. As Jesus hung on the cross, we're told that a large group of women who were with him in Galilee had accompanied him to Jerusalem (15:40–41). With this tiny comment, our whole mental picture of Jesus and his disciples is transformed; no longer should we imagine Jesus on the road with twelve men alone, but with a large mixed group, women as well as men. And the presence of these women might prompt us to ask other questions: what was their role? Should we assume it was any different from that of the men? Were they also preaching and healing? Did they perhaps have a mission to other *women*? In a society where men and women were strictly segregated, did these women teach and baptise their 'sisters' in the new faith? And is it precisely because they led a mission to other women that their contribution has been forgotten?

In the following chapters, we'll recover something of the history and activities of early Christian women in the earliest period of the new movement. We'll reveal as much as possible about the women who followed Jesus on the roads of Galilee or welcomed him into their homes, and reflect on how the memory of these women provided models as the Church spread across the world. Uncovering clues within the Gospel texts, we'll look at the named women around Jesus, seeing how they acted as disciples, apostles, healers and leaders, and we'll think about other unnamed women also. We'll see how women accompanied Jesus on his travels, and the pivotal role played by women like Mary Magdalene and Martha in communicating the message.

We'll begin by thinking about how these women have been remembered in ways that preserve them as important and yet also limit them, and will reflect on their presentation in the present day and through time, in art and early Christian literature as well as in the Gospels, and think about why this was. Only by understanding how and why stories about these women were preserved, changed or forgotten in the turns of time can we begin to make any proposals about who they really were. And we'll find evidence that allows us to glimpse them in their historical context, close to the side of Jesus.

We'll see too that women were associated with Paul and the spread of the new movement around the Mediterranean, acting as deacons, benefactors, leaders of house churches, teachers, healers, miracle-workers and missionaries. We'll look at women's activities in this slightly later period, raising them to visibility and restoring them and their stories to the historical record. As our journey progresses, we'll also look at how things changed for the worse for women – particularly in the more restrictive pastoral epistles (especially 1 and 2 Timothy), later additions to Paul's letters, and changes under the Roman emperor Constantine in the fourth century, when Christianity became the religion of the imperial house.

This book is written for non-specialists, for anyone interested in the early years of Christianity, and for women and men in today's churches with both an interest in their past and a concern for the future. It's written by two historians of early Christianity with a mission to disseminate the findings of feminist biblical scholars beyond the narrow confines of the academy. Much of what is in the book has been known by academics for some decades, though scholars are often bad at communicating their most interesting findings to the general public.

But the fault isn't entirely on the side of academics. Certain church groups have a vested interest in minimising the role of women in the foundations of Christianity. It's apparently easy for some people to be sniffy about feminist history, to say that there's no real evidence for women's activities or to accuse women of approaching the texts with their own, modern concerns. Needless to say, the writers of this book beg to differ.

Each of the key chapters treats a different female disciple or, occasionally, a group of women. It's not entirely exhaustive, but we've included nearly all the named women of the Gospels who have left some trace in the written records – and quite a few unnamed ones too. All together, they allow us to start to see something of the significant role played by women in the Jesus movement and the early church.

Where this book *is* distinctive is in the attention we pay to early non-biblical traditions about women that have survived in cultural memory – the vast store of tales, legends, hymns, iconography, commentaries, inscriptions and archaeological sites connected with female disciples of Jesus. In a society where no more than 10–15 per cent of people were literate, Christians would have encountered Jesus' earliest female disciples not only in the biblical texts that were read out at their gatherings, but also, and perhaps more intimately, in the liturgies, prayers and stories that told of their female forebears. In our own society, we tend to prize written texts above all else – to see them as authoritative and official – but within first-century culture the rich body of oral traditions was seen as equally valid and life-giving. Some early church scholars actively sought out the spoken word over written documents, living tradition in preference to cold text.

It's easy to dismiss this non-biblical material as derivative or legendary, nothing more than muddled memories, but we argue that it can contain within it echoes of women's past activity. These materials may have their own lines of transmission, some of them going back to the very earliest period. Just because they have no parallel in the Gospels does not necessarily count against them.

It's important to appreciate that for the first three centuries Christian tradition was fluid and unstable, with stories circulating in various different shapes and styles. Even Gospel texts and Pauline letters were frequently altered by copyists (sometimes deliberately so, as we'll see), and biblical scholars agree that the Gospels of Matthew, Luke and probably John are rewritings of Mark. They did not, however, simply replicate Mark word for word when they added their own material. Stories about Jesus and his first disciples were easily moulded to adapt to new situations, to respond to new challenges or to provide hope and encouragement in times of distress. Much would have circulated orally and might well have left no 'official' record. How much of this oral material has been completely forgotten is anyone's guess, though the likelihood is that much more has been forgotten than has been preserved – and some may have been deliberately suppressed.

All of this means that we have to be cautious in our reading of the biblical texts. As the decades passed and Christianity spread throughout the Mediterranean world, the new movement came under increasing pressure to conform to Roman society. This

The New Testament

Much of what we know about Jesus and his disciples comes from four Gospels that are included in the New Testament (the second part of the Christian Bible). These are the Gospels of Matthew, Mark, Luke and John. By the end of the second century, most mainstream Christians accepted that these were authoritative. Traditionally, they are associated with the authority of certain apostles (meaning 'envoys'): Mark is associated with the authority of Peter; Matthew and John were considered to be among Jesus' apostles; Luke was associated with the authority of Paul. However, today scholars debate the actual identities of the authors, because titles ascribing texts to certain authors were not always accurate. Also, it's clear that Matthew, Luke and John all used Mark (written c. 70 CE) in the creation of their own Gospels, which come from later decades.

These four Gospels are the only ones included in the New Testament 'canon' (literally meaning 'measure'), in that they measure up to a standard of theological correctness. But they were not the only ones in circulation during the first hundred years of the faith, and there were other early Christian writings that can shed important light on Jesus and his first followers.

meant, among other things, that Christian women had to be seen to know their place, to be submissive and to accept secondary roles. Where the biblical texts mention women, we always have to ask whether the author is describing women as they actually were, or as they would wish them to be. In other words, does a particular text mirror reality or attempt to transform it to outside expectations? When texts tell women to be silent or to learn submissively, we can be fairly sure that it implies the opposite – that some women are not doing these things! We have to be aware that stories and traditions involving women are very likely to have been forgotten or rewritten, tamed or domesticated.

In the following chapters, like detectives, we'll peel back the layers of the biblical stories and non-biblical traditions in an attempt to uncover something of the real, historical women behind the memories. We will give you our own translations of some key texts. Sometimes there's not much to go on and we'll need to use our imaginations, but carefully, fuelled by our knowledge of the past context in which these women lived and worked, and by a sense of what was possible or probable in an ancient society. At other times, there's more evidence and we'll catch occasional glimpses of the lives, hopes and activities of a range of different women right at the very beginning of Christian history. As one chapter builds on another, we aim to highlight the range of often surprising roles played by the women who knew Jesus.

Resetting our picture of early Christian women will transform our overall portrait of the early church. For some, this will be inspiring, an encouragement to find role models right at the very origins of their faith. For others, this will be deeply disturbing and unsettling. But the impact of Christian imagery doesn't stop at church doors. Paintings such as *The Last Supper*, with its all-male cast, go deep into our shared culture, providing pictorial archetypes of male-only gatherings, boardrooms or government cabinets. Changing our images from the past isn't just about justice for forgotten women of the first century, but for women's place throughout society. And as we'll see, women were at the table from the very beginning.

I

Women in the World of Jesus

Before we begin our journey back to the very beginnings of Christianity, we need to take a broader look at the ancient society into which it emerged. The new faith began in Judaea, in the far eastern part of both the Mediterranean and the Roman Empire. It's important to realise that there was no such thing as 'Christianity' at this early stage. Most of the women we'll meet in this book are Jewish, living either in the Jewish homeland of Judaea or in the Jewish communities found in all the major eastern cities of the Empire. As we follow the spread of the movement, we'll start to encounter pagan (or Gentile) women in these cities too. Technically speaking, all these women remained Jews or pagans, and are perhaps best described as 'Christ-confessing Jews/pagans'. But that's all a little cumbersome. We'll continue to use the term 'Christian' in this book, though readers should be aware that there's no sense in this early period of Christianity as a separate and clearly defined religion.

Although the Jewish way of life was distinctive in several ways, in broad terms Jewish women shared a common Mediterranean culture with their Roman sisters. Most basic here is the deeply patriarchal and hierarchical nature of society. The evidence for this is everywhere. Throughout the Roman Empire (Judaea as much as anywhere else), society in both cities and villages was organised around the rule of males, a method of organisation that was replicated in the smallest social unit of all, the household. The father (*paterfamilias*) was legally in charge, with the power to make a range of far-reaching decisions over his wife, family and slaves (if he had them). Men were expected to occupy public space such as courtrooms, schools and town or village assemblies. Women (unless slaves, prostitutes, rural workers or beggars) tended to occupy private space such as the home, where childrearing or caring for the elderly would take up much of their time, or to congregate as groups by rivers, where they might fetch water or do the family's washing, or to seek out the company of other women. These were general norms, despite some exceptions.

Life expectancy in the first century was frighteningly low, with relatively few people living much beyond forty years of age. Diseases such as dysentery, typhus, typhoid and tuberculosis were rife, along with malaria in certain areas. Starvation and malnutrition were widespread; even a minor infection could develop into a serious disability, and sickness and infirmity must have been everyday experiences. Female life expectancy was significantly shorter than that of men, with pregnancy and childbirth being particularly dangerous times. All of this led to a youthful population, though one in which sudden and unexplained death was an ever-present possibility, often disrupting family and household patterns.

A woman had little control over her own body and sexual preferences: marriage was usually arranged (or at least approved) by her father and frequently to an older man. A girl's first marriage would take place shortly after puberty, at early to mid-teens (the imbalance in age and experience would only strengthen the woman's secondary role in the relationship). Thereafter most women would expect to remarry if they were widowed, sometimes several times. After the age of thirty, however, a woman had little chance of remarrying, particularly once her childbearing years were over. Most women bore many children, but owing to the high childhood mortality rates (almost half of children died before their fifth birthday), families tended to be small. Divorce was common, in both Roman and Jewish society, though among Jews it could only be initiated by the man.

Overarching everything was a strong set of female ideals. Mediterranean society was largely driven by concepts of honour and shame. While men were particularly associated with the family honour or public esteem, acquired through keeping the family in check or success in business or public life, women were

Polygamy

While ancient Roman society was strictly monogamous, this was not the case in the Jewish world. Women could only have one husband, but a wealthy man could have as many wives as he liked (or could afford). Herod the Great, who was King of the Jews from 37–4 BCE, had ten wives, and the Jewish historian Josephus had four, of whom at least a couple may have been concurrent. In fact, a man was legally obliged to take his brother's wife as his own if his brother died childless. Any resulting children were said to belong to the dead brother. This was known as the law of Levirate marriage and could provide some protection for a widow (see Gen. 38:6–11; Deut. 25:5–10; the book of Ruth).

In 1960, archaeologists found a leather pouch containing personal documents from the early second century CE at the southern end of the Dead Sea. The documents related to a well-to-do woman named Babatha and included marriage contracts, records to do with the guardianship of minors and property transfers. Together they form a fascinating glimpse into one ancient woman's life. Babatha was married to a man called Jesus and had a son by him (also named Jesus). When he died, she married Judah, who already had a wife named Miriam and a teenage daughter called Shelamzion. What we don't know from all this is how the extended family arranged themselves – did they all live together, or in two parts of one house? The fact that Babatha and Miriam were embroiled in a legal argument over inheritance after Judah's death may suggest that relations weren't entirely harmonious between them earlier.

always a potential source of shame. A woman's failure to know her proper place or to assume too much authority over others, let alone socialising with other men than her husband or family members, could all bring shame on the family. The feminine ideal in this period was to support her husband, often to be dutiful and submissive, and to occupy herself with the raising of children and the smooth running of the home.

Women were expected to be chaste, modest and industrious. And although reality for most women was serial monogamy, there existed the ideal of the *univira*, the woman who refused to remarry and remained faithful to her husband even after his death. Conversely, the 'bad woman' spoke too much, had no sexual boundaries and challenged her husband's superiority. Men often assumed that women were gullible (particularly in the religious sphere) and prone to promiscuity (if given the chance) – though how far men really believed this to be true of their own mothers, wives and daughters is open to debate.

Of course, it's difficult to say how it 'felt' to be female in this society, and much depended on social status. Modern people might look back with horror at the constraints under which ancient women operated, and their lack of autonomy and opportunities. But we know that some found ways around society's limitations, using softer forms of influence, particularly in decisions affecting the home. Many women, for example, would have had a say in their daughters' marriage choices, or organised the running of their household in ways that suited them. While the henpecked husband was an object of ridicule, the very fact that such a character existed in comedies and histories alike suggests that some women did sometimes manage to exert their authority.

Issues of class and geographical location (particularly whether they were urban or rural) played a huge role in women's lives. Women of high status and independent means might enjoy a certain amount of freedom, especially if they were no longer married or caring for children or elderly relatives. In the Roman world, wealthy women attended dinner parties with their husbands and enjoyed a daily trip to the baths to relax and catch up on the news and gossip (though they'd be careful to protect their honour in the mixed facilities by taking their female slaves with them). Women could act as patrons of trade guilds and other associations, often in exchange for financial donations. The laws of reciprocity meant that in return for her patronage a woman would expect loyalty from the beneficiaries who would champion her concerns,

Women in the synagogue

Women participated alongside men in synagogue worship. Unlike the Jerusalem Temple, the synagogue was not considered to be sacred space or 'holy', but rather a place where people met to pray, read the Scriptures and discuss the Law. Some women may have read and led the prayers, especially if they occupied positions of leadership.

A number of inscriptions suggest that it was possible for women to act as the 'ruler of the synagogue'. It's not clear what this involved, though we might assume that it carried with it some kind of influence and status within the Jewish community, most likely in return for benefactions of some kind (financial or otherwise), and may have involved some kind of duties, perhaps planning the weekly service. The title could be used of men, women and children (such as Jairus in Mark 5:22, or the person who took issue with Jesus in the synagogue in Luke 13:10–17). When used of children, the title was probably hereditary or honorary in some way. It's been suggested that it was honorary in the case of women too, perhaps denoting the wife of the male leader of the synagogue (Mrs Vicar), but there is no good reason to support this, and the parallels with female pagan benefactors or priests would suggest that at least some women were able to hold this prestigious title in their own right.

A second-century inscription from Smyrna (in western Asia Minor) proclaims that a Jewish woman named Rufina built a tomb for her slaves and freedpersons. Clearly, she was a wealthy, independent woman (there's no mention of a husband or father); she acts as a benefactor and identifies herself as the leader of the synagogue:

> *The Jew Rufina, ruler of the synagogue, built this tomb for her freedpersons and her slaves. None other has the right to bury a body here. If, however, anyone shall have the boldness to do so, they must pay 1,500 denarii into the holy treasury and 1,000 denarii to the Jewish people. A copy of this inscription has been deposited in the archives.*

provide whatever services she needed and publicly honour her name. There is archaeological evidence to show that women served as priestesses of pagan cults, and Jewish women could attain the rank of 'ruler of synagogue'. These were sometimes honours bestowed on wealthy, high-status women because of financial benefactions, including funding buildings. But still, there was considerable authority that came with such honours. And although literacy rates were very low in this period – probably fewer than 10–15 per cent of people could read – we do sometimes hear of elite women receiving an education.

Lower down the social scale, women had jobs. We find them in a range of activities: engaging in trade and working in market stalls and shops, baking and weaving, leasing property or running inns, and even working as blacksmiths or painters (though in all these they usually worked alongside their husbands or fathers in a family business). Rural women living at or around subsistence level might find themselves working alongside the men in the fields, tending the animals, working the olive presses or collecting the grape or date harvest, depending on the most pressing needs. We'll see in the next chapter that fisherwomen on the Sea of Galilee took on a variety of roles, from gutting fish to mending nets, arranging the payment of taxes and distribution of the catch. And most of these women would have assisted their friends and neighbours, acting as midwives, wet nurses or hairdressers. As we shall begin to appreciate in the following chapters, women's experiences were many and varied.

Slavery was also common at this time, among Jews as well as pagans, and was rarely questioned. It's been estimated that as much as one-third of the population of Italy were slaves, with the rest of the Empire averaging around 10 per cent. People might be born into slavery (in the master's home) or be sold into slavery as prisoners of war or because of debt. Roman society practised infanticide, where unwanted babies were exposed – often on the rubbish heaps – and this was another source of slaves, particularly girls, who were seen as a poorer investment than their brothers. Although Jewish writers condemned the practice, it seems to have been common enough in the pagan cities, with rescued girls later put to work as prostitutes.

Slaves were the property of their masters and were often badly treated; it was simply assumed that female (and male) slaves were sexually available both to the master of the household and to anyone else to whom he wanted to lend them. Slaves could marry other slaves (though the marriages were not formally recognised), and any children who survived would automatically become the property of the owner.

Slave women had a particularly hazardous existence, especially as they aged and became less attractive or unable to work. Sometimes, however, slaves were freed by their owners; while this was often a benefit to male slaves who were able to use their former connections to do well in the world, it tended to be less advantageous to women, who frequently ended up working as prostitutes or becoming beggars.

In the religious sphere, texts and inscriptions from all over the early Roman Empire offer us a picture of a lively, varied and often competitive religious marketplace. Established cults and rituals vied with new cults and patterns of worship, new ideas about the divine and all kinds of wandering philosophers, healers and other miracle workers. There seems to have been a widely shared openness to new cults, communities and religious practitioners, and a frequent appetite for new religious leaders, new worshipping communities and new forms of religious life. This openness meant that Judaism itself was attractive to non-Jews in the cities in the eastern Mediterranean.

It was in this variegated context that Christianity first spread and took root. As we'll see, the new faith appealed to women at every level of society, just as it did to men. But before we can start to meet them, we need to say a few very general things about the earliest Christians and the language used to describe their leaders.

The first believers

The term for 'church' in Greek is *ekklesia*, which means 'assembly'. This was the term used for the assembly of Israel in the Greek version of the Jewish Scriptures. The first Christians met together in local groups, believing they were also part of something much greater. However, the church didn't come along fully formed with a clear organisational structure. Quite the reverse. In the earliest period, our texts make it clear that these small gatherings of believers fervently expected Jesus' imminent return on the clouds of glory and the transformation of the age. They were convinced that they were living at the end of the era and that their mission was to spread the message as widely as possible. In that context, there was no need for organisational structures or a fixed leadership – things were much more fluid and informal. As the decades wore on, however, it became clear that Jesus wasn't going to return as soon as they'd imagined, and this realisation led them to work out strategies for survival in an often hostile and unfriendly Roman world. Unsurprisingly, perhaps, there was a great deal of diversity in all this, with different places adopting different tactics, depending on local conditions.

In this period of change and evolution we see the emergence and development of key leadership roles within Christian gatherings – bishop/overseer (*episkopos*), elder/priest (*presbuteros*) and deacon/minister (*diakonos*) – though exactly what these roles entailed is hard to pin down; quite possibly they functioned differently in different contexts. We also hear of prophets, apostles and teachers (see 1 Cor. 12). Later church records give the impression that these roles were always held by men, but both texts and inscriptional evidence – as well as artistic representations – indicate that this wasn't the whole story. While in a gendered world it was expected that men would usually hold positions of responsibility, we've already seen that women could hold important roles in synagogues, temples and elsewhere.

Early Christianity was very diverse and widespread across the Mediterranean and Middle East by the end of the second century.

There were some Christians who clearly had women leaders (such as so-called Marcionite, Montanist and Gnostic groups), but even in the mainstream churches, what we call the 'proto-orthodox' types, the evidence suggests that women continued to exercise key ministries. We also hear of specifically female orders of widows and virgins: celibate women who were independent and autonomous. What we see is a suppression of women's leadership within the mainstream/proto-orthodox type of Christianity.

Why did this happen? While women's involvement in the mission of Jesus and the early church is a matter of celebration for women in the twenty-first century, the same wasn't true for the early church. As far as opponents of Christianity in the first centuries of our era were concerned, the obvious presence and leadership of women in the churches was a reason to dismiss the entire movement as completely pathetic. In a man's world, with endemic patriarchy, women leaders were not exemplary, unless they were the mothers, wives or daughters of important men, or else queens or empresses or other high-status women who performed masculine roles in some way. The presence of women in the generally non-elite Christian movement – they assumed – only went to show that it was disreputable, scandalous, and even downright dangerous and subversive (since having women in charge clearly went against the natural laws of nature). We have plenty of cases of eminent men sneering at Christians by pointing to the prominent role of women. The philosophers Celsus and Porphyry assumed that they could dismiss the credibility of the new faith simply by highlighting the surprisingly high level of women's involvement.

The problem with women

The philosopher Celsus (c.170 CE) wrote an entire treatise attacking Christians, in which he states:

> *Do you think that the ending of your tragedy is to be thought of as noble and convincing ... that while alive he (Jesus) was no*

---

help to himself, but dead he rose, and showed the signs of his punishment [and how his hands were pierced?]. Who saw this? A delirious (paroistros) woman as you say, and someone else from the same sorcery.

(Origen, Contra Celsum 2:55)

The Christians won over 'idiotic, low-class and stupid people, with women and children' (Origen, Contra Celsum *3:44, 49). They performed 'tricks in market-places' and got hold of 'children and women as ignorant as themselves' who then had to 'leave their father and their teachers, and go with the women and their playfellows to the women's apartments, or to the shoemaker's, or to the fuller's shop, so that they may attain perfection' (Origen,* Contra Celsum *3:55). The Christians even had whole groups who followed women teachers: 'There are Marcellians, so called from Marcellina, and Harpocratians from Salome, and others who derive their name from Mariamme, and others again from Martha' (Origen,* Contra Celsum *5:62). What a disastrous lot they were!*

Around the same time, Lucian of Samosata, in The Passing of Peregrinus, *wrote of 'old hag widows and orphaned children' looking after his Christian anti-hero. Another philosopher, Porphyry (c.280* CE*) wrote that the 'senate' (leadership) of Christians is in the hands of women (Jerome,* Comm in Jes. *3:12).*

In this environment, is it any wonder that Christian authors preferred to push back and relate and preserve the stories of (reliable) men, even though society at large could see women at the forefront of the movement? Pliny the Younger, a Roman governor in Bithynia and Pontus on the Black Sea, wrote to Emperor Trajan in the year 112 CE *about how he arrested two female slaves, who were* ministreae *(ministers = deacons) in the local church. He wanted to know what they were doing in their meetings, and had them thoroughly tortured to find out.*

The natural response to this on the part of Christian writers was to downplay women's activities, and to suggest that those women who did join the movement were eminently respectable (we'll see later that this strategy was used by the authors of Luke's Gospel and the pastoral epistles in particular). Our approach in this book is to seek to raise women to visibility when much evidence has been lost. Given that the rhetorical direction of our texts is towards downplaying women's contributions, we can be sure that what echoes remain are hints of something much bigger. We're quite well aware that the texts – whether Gospels, Pauline letters or other early Christian literature – were not written to furnish us with details of women's lives, experiences and contributions. Yet if we look carefully, we can gather a certain number of clues that point to a whole story of women's involvement in early Christian history – a story that has rarely been told outside academic circles.

Another difficulty here is language itself. We ourselves had a strange experience when making our documentary, *Jesus' Female Disciples*. We were talking to some young Bedouin men in Jordan. One man told us that he had eight brothers, though as the conversation continued it became clear that he included sisters in his tally of 'brothers'. Clearly, in Arabic the masculine term 'brothers' can include siblings of either gender (rather like the French *fils* which includes men and women). Greek, too, the language of the New Testament and early Christian texts, tends to mask the presence of women with male-gendered terms. When Paul speaks to his 'brothers', *adelphoi*, then, we can't assume that he is speaking to an all-male crowd: it should correctly be translated as 'siblings', or 'brothers and sisters'.

There are many instances in Greek where we can see that the term includes women. It's even demonstrated in an Alexandrian coin (third century BCE) where the word *adelphōn* '[coin] of [the] siblings' is written above the heads of brother and sister co-regents, King and Queen Ptolemy II Philadelphus and Arsinoe II.

Fortunately, this has been recognised by many (but not all) modern translations of the New Testament, which render *adelphoi* as used by Paul as 'brothers and sisters' in English. The fact is that the masculine plural of words like *adelphoi*, 'siblings', or *mathētai*, 'disciples', in Greek implicitly includes women. Even if men were in the minority in a room, the masculine plural would be used. The feminine plural would only be used if there were no men present. In what follows, then, we shall always ask whether women's involvement has simply been masked by grammatical constructions, so that a masculine plural in Greek has been read to indicate a masculine reality. We always have to think: women were there too.

Finally, it's worth highlighting a number of terms that will come up frequently in this book. One is the difference between a disciple and an apostle. Disciples (from the Latin *discipuli*) were those who would learn from a philosophical teacher. They were students who would sit at the feet of a teacher and study. They were supposed to offer service to their teacher in return for their education, and to treat their teacher as their 'master'. Once adept in the teaching, they were expected to be able to pass it on to others.

Disciples don't seem to have been particularly common in the Old Testament (though Elijah had Elisha, and there are some references to other prophets having a band of disciples); they do, however, seem to have been prominent in the Graeco-Roman world of the New Testament, where philosophers commonly attracted a group of disciples.

While disciples were frequently male, we do hear of female ones too. Plato, for example, was said to have had two women in his group of companions, Pythagoras also attracted female disciples, and the Theban philosopher Crates was followed by Hipparchia (who eventually married him). In terms of the Gospels, disciples are also understood as followers, and Jesus is shown as calling his first disciples by explicitly asking them to 'follow me'. Following Jesus meant a total commitment to his teaching and his lifestyle.

Apostles (from the Greek *apostello*, 'send out') are people sent out for a specific task as envoys of someone. Apostles, or envoys, of Jesus would first have been disciples, but then – once proficient enough – they could be sent out to represent Jesus. In the early

Christian world, we will meet both men and women who are referred to as 'apostles', people sent out to spread the message.

It's easy to confuse the term 'apostle' and 'disciple', and indeed the Gospel of Matthew shapes Mark's tradition to simplify things in this direction. The key thing is that many people can become disciples (or followers) and live in commitment to a specific teaching, but only some get 'sent out' as envoys to spread the message of the teacher.

One last term is 'minister', *diakonos*, which comes from the Greek verb *diakoneo*, 'minister, serve', from which we get the English 'deacon'. What's intriguing about this term is that when it's used of a male it tends to be translated as 'ministered' in ways that suggest a church office, such as 'acted as a deacon'. When used of women, however, it tends to be translated at best as 'deaconess' (a lower order in some churches) or more commonly as 'serve at tables', 'take care of' or 'provide food for'. We will find this word applied to many early Christian women, but we'll not assume that only domestic activities are meant, particularly when it is clear from the context that other translations are more appropriate.

In what follows, we'll base our reconstructions on a variety of material – from the texts of the New Testament to later writings that weren't included and from literary evidence to art and archaeology. Later texts provide excellent clues to how Jesus' female disciples were remembered over time, and what kinds of models they provided for women in churches throughout the Graeco-Roman world. With all this in mind, it's time to meet our earliest female disciples of Jesus.

2

Salome and 'Many Others'

There were also women looking on from a distance; among whom were also Mary Magdalene, and Mary the mother of James the younger and of Joses, and Salome. These used to follow him and minister to him when he was in Galilee; and there were *many other women* who had come up with him to Jerusalem.

(Mark 15:40–41)

We've already seen that Mark rather belatedly – at the crucifixion! – remembers to tell us that 'many other women' had journeyed with Jesus from Galilee to Jerusalem. In contemporary culture, the very existence of these women – let alone their names – has been all but forgotten. TV documentaries, films and art all depict Jesus surrounded by twelve men, only occasionally remembering to include Mary Magdalene in the group, and rarely any other women.

So who were the 'many' others? One female disciple who attracted attention in the early church was Salome, who is mentioned explicitly only in Mark (as part of the group of female disciples at the cross, and later at the empty tomb). It is expected that the audience will recognise her name, though, as we'll see, the other Gospels either refer to her in a different way or choose to note the presence of other women instead. She's mentioned in passing in a range of early Christian literature, often alongside Mary Magdalene as the foremost female disciple.

From ancient ossuaries (bone boxes) and inscriptions we know that the name Salome was very common in the first century (second only to Mary), and so she is often confused with the Salome who appeared at the birth of Jesus in the *Protoevangelium of James*, or the dancing daughter of Herodias (whom Josephus names Salome). More commonly in mainstream tradition she is identified as the mother of the sons of Zebedee, Mary the wife of Clopas or even the sister of Jesus. But what are the most accurate memories? In our quest to uncover Salome and her many female companions, and to work out why they devoted their lives to Jesus and his mission, we need to go back to the very beginning of the movement, to the Sea of Galilee.

Fishers of people

It's clear from the Gospels that Jesus' earliest disciples were men and women from the fishing industry around the Sea of Galilee. A well-worn track linked Nazareth with the towns and villages on the western shore of the lake: Capernaum, Bethsaida, Tarichaea, Tiberias and others. Although some of these – such as Capernaum – were poor, largely built out of black, basalt field stones, archaeological excavations have shown that others were reasonably prosperous towns, where a successful local elite followed the architectural fashions of the Empire, even if most of the inhabitants made do with a more basic standard of life.

Contrary to much popular opinion, not all fisherfolk were poor, eking out a living around the lake. In the first century, fishing was a thriving industry on the shore where fresh fish were dried, salted and often turned into garum (the ancient equivalent of ketchup) and exported all over the Empire. Fish bones are commonly found on archaeological sites, suggesting that fresh fish was quickly sent to market and consumed across a wide local area. And while it would be wrong to describe any ancient worker as 'rich' or 'prosperous' by our standards, those engaged in the fishing industry could have enjoyed a moderate income and a comfortable lifestyle well above that of an agricultural worker.

Fishing was highly regulated, with the right to fish controlled by the ruler; in Galilee, this meant Herod Antipas, the son of Herod the Great, who ruled from 4 BCE to 39 CE. Families or consortia would lease sections of the coastline for their boats

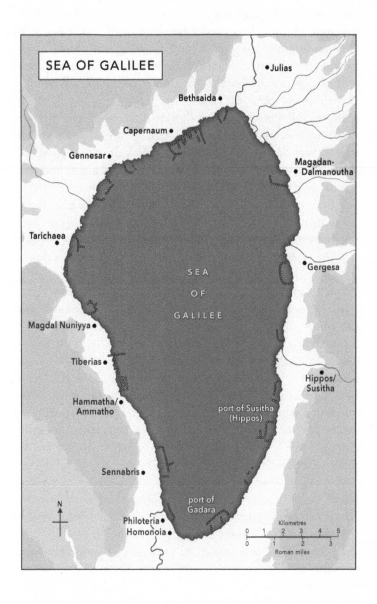

(which they might own or hire), and local supervisors and taxmen would monitor the day's catch as it was brought in. The Gospels allow us to glimpse the Zebedee family at work on the Sea, with the father and his two sons in the boat along with hired hands. Another set of brothers, Peter and Andrew, may have been part of the same consortium, pooling their resources to buy a boat or to share labour and transport costs.

Surprisingly, perhaps, fisherfolk were at the centre of a complex web of connections. They needed boats, nets, lead weights, stone anchors, floats, hooks, ropes, baskets and all the other parapher-nalia of their trade. Some of this was local – linen nets and sails, for example, were manufactured locally – but some needed to come from a distance. The Ginosar boat, found in the lake during a drought in 1986, was made of cedar wood, which must have been imported from the Lebanon mountains some 70–100km away. Those engaged in the fishing industry also needed access to transport to take fresh fish to market, and processing facilities to salt it for wider export. The lake would have been a busy centre of activity and industry, and a hub of social, administrative and legal connections. In the Gospels Jesus seems at home in this environment and may well have been connected with the fishing industry himself – perhaps as a boat builder?

As always in antiquity, there would have been a clear division of labour. The menfolk went out to fish, hauling in the nets from the boat or along the shore. When the boats were damaged, they likely mended them themselves: the Ginosar boat shows evidence of many repairs, the amateurish nature of which suggests that they are the handiwork of the fishermen rather than professional boat builders. The Gospels suggest that men mended nets too; since these were made of linen, they had the advantage of becoming almost invisible in the water, though they broke easily and needed constant repair.

Writers on the ancient fishing industry often wonder who gutted the fish and prepared them for market. Comparison with the fishing industry off the eastern coast of Scotland suggests one very obvious answer: the wives, sisters and daughters! No doubt they sorted and prepared the fish and packaged them for sale. Some might also have taken on a variety of other roles, from mending nets to paying the taxmen, and constantly maintaining all-important connections with other women around the lake.

We shouldn't entertain too many romantic notions about all this: it would have been hard labour, always working to a deadline to get the catch to its destination before it went off, and income may not always have been spread around fairly. Women's hands would have been continually cut by the bony fish and the sharp knives that they needed for their trade, while younger children and elderly relatives endlessly needed a watchful eye.

Once news of Jesus' mission reached the lake, it would have spread quickly along well-established networks – not just to other fisherfolk but also to suppliers, traders, hired workmen and tax and government officials (it is no surprise to find taxmen among Jesus' first disciples). Women would have shared stories with other women as they gutted the fish, anxious for new reports as friends and acquaintances bustled around the lakeshore, a sense of growing excitement over everything. Only a short while earlier, John

---

Women's clothes

Let's imagine our women. Clothes in the ancient Mediterranean world were not just about practicality but they also sent out important messages about the wearer's status and marital situation. Despite the hot summers, layers were definitely in. For a woman there was a thin undertunic, often made of one piece. The basic outer garment was quite a wide tunic, which was secured at the shoulders (either by sewing, or by brooches) and belted under the breasts. Sleeves were formed by the overhang of the cloth from the shoulders, and usually just reached the elbows. This outer garment often reached the feet, commonly with two narrow stripes from each shoulder to hem.

On the eastern side of the Mediterranean, including in Judaea, ordinary women wore a shawl over their heads (see page 29). Wealthy women favoured large mantles in fine fabrics, wrapped around them to show their refined modesty and to cover their heads and arms more voluminously. Poor women

also wore mantles for warmth, but otherwise kept their arms free for work.

A wide range of fabrics could be used in dressmaking – linen, wool, goat hair or silk – but in Judaea most fabric was made of wool. While natural dyes were cheapest, the rich could signal their wealth by dressing in certain types of purple, blue or crimson. Natural dyes also produced bright colours, and archaeological finds show how the common people of Judaea loved such hues: mainly bright reds, yellows, oranges and greens. This was not a beige world: only men and women of certain philosophical schools rejected colour to dress in undyed or white fabric, and that stood out as distinctly different. Men were expected to be more muted in their colour tastes, unless they were wishing to advertise their wealth or status, of course.

Most clothing was made from simple shapes – usually rectangles – so that pieces were easy to make and there was little waste. Lower-class women would weave their own fabrics and make their own clothes, while those higher up the social ladder could afford ornate fabrics made by skilled weavers, and professionally made outfits. A good piece of clothing was a valuable item, and pieces were often passed down through the family or sold as second-hand. Even old pieces of cloth were valuable and could be used as rags, for example for mending, cleaning, menstruation, nappies and for wrappers (there were no paper or plastic bags in antiquity!).

On a less pleasant note, hair and body lice were common problems, and were found on ancient combs and clothing. Getting rid of the parasites was difficult, particularly for poorer people who might only have one undergarment.

Free women and girls would usually wear jewellery, either fancy gold and jewels for high-class wealthy women, or else simple glass and stone beads for the poor. Cosmetics were also used – strong eyebrows were highly fashionable, along with eyeshadow and face creams to even out the complexion and hide blemishes (though some of the latter contained lead and other substances that did more harm than good).

The dress of women in first-century Judaea

the Baptist had called people to go out to him at the River Jordan
to wash away their sins by repentance and immersion, to prepare
themselves for God's imminent arrival, purified and ready. Perhaps
many of the women had gone out to see him along with their
menfolk, and even been baptised themselves.

But Jesus was different. He didn't base himself in the wilderness, expecting people to come out to him. Instead, he found
people in their own environments, in the towns and villages of
Galilee. And while he had a wonderful message about the kingdom of God, what would really have attracted the crowds would
have been his amazing ability as a healer and exorcist. As we've
already seen, disease was very common in the first century, including leprosy and other skin diseases. On the low-lying shores of the
lake, malaria was appallingly common, and ill health and disability
would have been familiar among rich and poor alike. In a world
where doctors were rare (and affordable by only the rich), most
people had to make do with little more than traditional remedies
and folk medicine – potions made from medicinal herbs or roots
– and amulets. Women in particular were often drawn to the
healing arts, as midwives or 'wise women'.

It's easy to imagine the excitement along the lake as ever more
reports told of incredible healings in the nearby villages. Even

Jesus' enemies could not deny that he was a particularly gifted and effective healer; their only explanation was that he was some kind of a sorcerer, channelling the power of evil spirits.

Enthusiasm would only have increased as people met Jesus along the shore or went out to listen to him themselves and saw his abilities first-hand. The growing crowds who came to see marvellous acts of healing doubtless stayed to hear what Jesus had to say. They would have heard his call for repentance and his promise of the imminent arrival of God's kingdom, a new world characterised by righteousness, toleration and equality of all. Women would have found this message as attractive as men would have. In Jesus they saw someone whose authority wasn't derived from the traditional bodies of power – the Temple, legal schools and priesthood – but someone like them, someone whose possession by God's Spirit gave him extraordinary powers to heal and to prophesy.

The first disciples of Jesus weren't just the poor and outcast, but were largely drawn from those who had something to give up (homes, families, livelihoods). Nor were they necessarily people who felt excluded and oppressed by society. Their encounter with Jesus, however, forcefully opened their eyes to the possibilities of God's love in their lives, and the need for renewal and change. Some of them were seized by the desire to become more involved and to follow Jesus, dropping out of society and working to establish a new world while they waited for God to establish it with power.

Women with children or elderly relatives to care for would have needed to stay at home; the demands of dependants would have been too great simply to abandon. Some may have seen their husbands go after Jesus. Would they have encouraged them, or resented their freedom? Life would have been incredibly difficult with no man to take the boats out and no assured income. It's hard to imagine the male disciples abandoning their families without making some kind of provision for them. We might hope that wider family, friends and neighbours rallied round and offered them work somewhere along the fish production process. We'll see later on that some wealthier members of the movement, particularly women, may have used their assets to alleviate the poverty of those left behind (see Chapter 3 on Joanna).

If it was within these communities that Jesus found his first male disciples, it seems very likely that at least some of the 'many women' who followed him were also to be found here. Some of them were probably relatives of the men. Church tradition suggests that Jesus' sisters were among the disciples (see the fourth-century *Apostolic Constitutions* 3:6, while the third-century Valentinian Gnostic *Gospel of Philip* mentions a sister named Mary, 59:6–11). Others may have been relatives of the first male disciples. Perhaps some were mothers, wives, sisters or cousins of Peter, Andrew, James and John.

What's the big deal with the 'Twelve'?

The number twelve had great symbolic value, corresponding to the twelve tribes of Israel (Num. 1:4–16), named in accordance with the twelve sons of Israel: the tribes of Judah, Simeon, Levi, Benjamin, Naphtali, Dan and so on. Ten tribes had been swept away in the Assyrian invasion in the eighth century BCE, leaving only two tribes by the time of Jesus – Judah and Benjamin, along with the priestly tribe of Levi.

By sending out the Twelve as apostles ('envoys'), listed as named men, Jesus symbolically declared the renewal of Israel, as it had been in the glory days of David and Solomon. In this renewal, though, the Twelve were actually defined as judges of the twelve tribes: 'in the regeneration, when this human son will sit on his glorious throne, you who have followed me will sit on twelve thrones judging the twelve tribes of Israel' (Matt. 19:28). Because of this role, as Acts tells it, the eleven apostles looked for a replacement for Judas soon after the resurrection (see Acts 1:21). But this charged symbolism of the Twelve should not confuse us into thinking the apostles were men who worked alone or that being an apostle was an exclusively male role. It's clear that Jesus had other disciples alongside the Twelve. The model of a named male envoy working with a female partner, which is found or implied in our early evidence, asks us to think more about how the Twelve (or even Jesus) operated in practice, and the appointment of seventy or seventy-two further apostles (as recorded in Luke) leaves open all kinds of possibilities for alternative identities and partnerships for people going on missions.

Early on we hear that Jesus healed Peter's mother-in-law from a fever (perhaps malaria) at Peter's house in Capernaum (Matt. 8:14–15). Once healed, we're told, she 'ministered to them'. In the context, this clearly means that she showed her gratitude by providing hospitality to Jesus and his companions. But it's quite possible that she became a disciple too and took to the road with Jesus and the others, now 'ministering' along with the other women.

Perhaps this woman's daughter, Peter's wife, also accompanied Peter when he was sent out by Jesus. Paul stated in his first letter to the Corinthian Church that he surely had the right to a 'sister woman/wife like Cephas, the [male] apostles and brothers of the Lord' (1 Cor. 9:5). 'Cephas' is another way of referring to Peter, since *Kepha* in Aramaic means the same as *Petros* in Greek, both meaning 'rock'. Paul was saying that other male apostles had female companions with them in the work. After all, it was the role of wives (and slaves) to provide *diakonia*, 'ministry' or 'service', as Josephus noted (*Antiquities* 18:21). A 'sister' implies fellow discipleship.

Paul's words give us an impression of a pattern of a team of male and female apostolic pairs, like Prisca and Aquila (Acts 18:2). But these pairs may not always have been married couples. His statement connects well with a mention of Jesus' first envoys in Galilee, the Twelve, going off 'two [by] two' (*duo duo*, Mark 6:7). This is a peculiar expression found famously in the Greek version of Genesis 6–7 in relation to animals – male and female – going into Noah's ark, and is not the usual way of referring to people being grouped in pairs (in this case, pairs of men). As in the children's song, 'The animals went in two by two, hoorah, hoorah', the implication is of male–female pairs, and the equivalent expression is used in Hebrew in the Dead Sea Scrolls to mean exactly that. It subtly implies that the twelve named men (from Simon Peter to Judas Iscariot) went out around Galilee with 'sister wives' (female companions).

As we have seen, in Mark, the female disciples of Jesus are hidden until they are needed to witness the crucifixion, and we may speculate on the reasons. Maybe this is because the focus of the Gospel is on showing how the twelve male apostles failed.

Jesus sent them out with precious little, seeking the compassion-ate welcome of strangers in the villages they entered (6:8–11). Rather than humbly establishing a new Israel by their loving actions of healing and proclamation, they misunderstood Jesus and let him down (e.g., 4:41; 5:31; 6:52; 8:4, 21; 14:50). They wanted to know who was the greatest, at which Jesus picked up a child (from among his disciples in the house) and stated, 'Anyone who welcomes one of such children in my name welcomes me' (9:37). This is sometimes presented as if Jesus was saying people should be nice to children. However, since Jesus had sent his apostles out in his name to be so welcomed, he seemed to be clas-sifying a child as his greatest representative. In this case, when we think of the apostles going out 'two by two', male and female, we should probably also think of the children they could at times take with them.

The whole notion of 'ministry' or 'service', the usual preserve of women and slaves, was totally turned around by Jesus, who said to the Twelve, 'If anyone wants to be first, they shall be the last of everyone, and server (*diakonos*) of everyone' (Mark 9:35), and, 'Whoever wants to be great among you will be your server' (10:43). Jesus himself was 'one who serves' (10:44–45). It looks a lot like Jesus was modelling himself on women and slaves, but his service as shown in the Gospels was actually often about healing. He was able to cure people and he attracted huge crowds as a result.

Healing was always a big part of the mission of Jesus and his early apostles (envoys). They were supposed to spread his message, anoint people with oil and heal (Mark 6:6–13). We can link this back to the implied presence of women disciples engaged in this important mission, as they all went out 'two by two'. Women were surely serving Jesus in his service along with the men, and were needed in a very gendered society, to anoint the women with oil and heal.

So when the women who followed Jesus in Galilee are said to 'minister', 'provide for' or 'serve' him (15:41), we need to imagine a wide range of activities they could have been doing, furthering the service of Jesus himself. They are the other half of the story of

Jesus and the Twelve, even though they are largely veiled from view.

Companies of male and female travellers, old and young, children included, were comparatively well known, particularly at Passover when groups of pilgrims would make their way from Galilee to Jerusalem for the feast. These groups would largely be composed of extended families and neighbours, ensuring that their association wouldn't arouse criticism and incur shame on the women present. This would have been a safe way for women to travel, whether married or not. Jesus' disciples understood themselves collectively as a big family group, referring to each other as sisters and brothers. As Jesus said, looking around at his mixed group of disciples, 'Whoever does the will of God is my brother and my sister and my mother (Mark 3:35). Jesus taught the will of God to his disciples and saw them all as his family of faith. This created a proclamation about their identity, and almost dared anyone to think otherwise.

As the group made its way around Galilee, it presumably attracted others. We'll meet Joanna in the next chapter, a woman who seems to have been of high status. In Luke, a woman named Susanna is mentioned (Luke 8:3), though nothing more is known of her. Some of these women may have been older widows with nothing to keep them at home; others may have been freed-women, or even runaway servants or slaves.

Eating with Jesus

The Gospels record a confrontation between Jesus and the Pharisees (a respected legal school) about eating practices. They accused Jesus of eating with 'tax collectors and sinners' (see, for example, Mark 2:15–17), to which Jesus replied that a doctor needs to go not to the healthy but to the sick – meaning, of course, that his mission was to those who weren't regarded as pious by people such as the Pharisees. In a passage only found in Matthew's Gospel, however, Jesus linked tax collectors with prostitutes, suggesting that both groups had gone out to John the

Baptist and that both groups would be among the first to enter the kingdom of God, ahead of his Pharisaic accusers (Matt. 21:31–32). It's difficult to know what to make of this, but one possibility is that Jesus himself was criticised for associating not only with 'tax collectors and sinners' but also with prostitutes. If so, this may be an echo of a slur cast over the women of his group.

But why would anyone want to label them as prostitutes? We need to remember that the term *pornai* (usually translated as 'prostitutes') is in Greek a much broader expression than 'sex-workers'. In Hebrew and Aramaic, a *zonah* is a sexually immoral woman, more like a 'slut' or 'slag' in colloquial British English. Linked with a verb that means 'to run off', it could refer to an adulteress or any female transgressor of sexual norms – wayward women in general. Some of the rabbinic sages included in this category any girls or women who were not able to have children ('barren'), and others included proselytes (converts to Judaism), freed slaves or those who had engaged in any kind of forbidden sexual relationship (see the Mishnah, tractate Yebamoth 6:5). While the women disciples of Jesus may have been hailed by him as his sisters, sceptical onlookers would have judged differently.

The women disciples of Jesus may also have been genuinely identified as besmirched for their previous transgressions. The Gospel tradition gives us two different stories of women who were 'sinners' who were not judged and condemned by Jesus, as expected, but forgiven. In the one case, Jesus challenged men about to stone an adulteress that the one without sin among them should cast the first stone (John 8:7), and they all stopped one by one and left. In the other story, Jesus acknowledged the exemplary love shown by a woman deemed a 'sinner' who should not have touched him, when she was forgiven (Luke 7:36–50).

Even for hitherto respectable women, mixing in this new family of brothers and sisters had its pitfalls in terms of public perception. Faced with being labelled as a 'prostitute', women might well have thought twice about whether to join Jesus' band of disciples. This was not an era in which most women were expected to make autonomous decisions about their lives. People lived in extended family groups in which their role was an essential part of the social unit. A girl or woman was under the authority of the male head of household, as we noted above.

The context of shared meals may give us a clue as to how they could be judged. It was common in Roman times for well-to-do Roman matrons to attend dinner parties with their husbands, though they would usually sit on a chair rather than recline on a couch, as the latter was associated with 'prostitutes'. These shared meals were widespread and might have taken place in other people's homes or in local clubs or trade associations. It's unlikely that the niceties of table etiquette were followed by Jesus' Galilean disciples, and in any case it was standard Jewish practice for women to recline alongside the men at the Sabbath meal and at Passover (both of which were family meals). Whether or not Jesus and his disciples actually 'reclined' as they ate together, their shared meal with no differentiation between the sexes – while of no particular note to most observers – might have caught the eye of some wealthier Pharisaic opponents who might then have used it as ammunition in their attacks on Jesus and his group. Of course, this is the oldest trick in the book: the Pharisees were not interested in the women themselves, but used them as a way to get at Jesus. A teacher who associates with tax collectors, sinners and prostitutes – they argued – can hardly be trusted.

It's possible, then, that there was a touch of scandal associated with the women around Jesus, though this was spread about by opponents. Even without rumour and insinuation, however, life on the road would have been difficult for these women. They were exposed to the dangers of robbers and wild animals, not to mention cold nights when they were unable to find hospitality. They may well have used their connections from the fishing industry to link up with networks all over Galilee, seeking out those they had traded with or met at the market in each new town. And, of course, women who wanted to know more about Jesus and his movement would first make contact with them, finding their company a safer way to start their journey than with the men.

Many Marys

It can sometimes seem as if nearly all the women in the Gospels and Acts were called Mary. Strange as it may seem, historians estimate that almost half of women in the first century were called Mary. This is why they needed nicknames, or to be identified according to their fathers, husbands and sons (for example, Mary Magdalene and Mary the mother of Jesus). A second very common name was Salome. Both names were associated with the Hasmonaean dynasty, Jewish monarchs of the second–first century BCE. Salome was the name of a Jewish Queen who reigned from 76–67 BCE, while Mary was a version of Mariamme (or Miriam), the name of Herod I's favourite wife. Given their association with the past, the two names may have evoked a nostalgia for Jewish home rule and encouraged some to dream of national independence once again.

Salome

It's often supposed that Mark's Salome was the mother of the Zebedee brothers. Indeed, she is remembered as the mother of the sons of Zebedee in the Eastern Orthodox Church, and commemorated on 3 August. The reason for this is because once the four Gospels were collected together in books, in the later second and third centuries, people started to read one Gospel in the light of another. In Mark 15:40–41, there are three women:

- Mary Magdalene
- Mary the mother of James the less and Joses
- Salome

In Matthew, however, Salome is omitted, and we find a reference instead to 'the mother of Zebedee's children' (Matt. 27:56). One obvious way to reconcile the two accounts is to suggest that Salome was in fact the mother of James and John. Earlier in Matthew, this same woman asked Jesus if her sons could sit in the seats of honour in his kingdom (Matt. 20:20). In its context, this is clearly an attempt to deflect any criticism for this embarrassing request away from James and John (who asked Jesus for the honourable seats themselves in Mark 10:35–40). But the passage is located as the group makes its way down to Jerusalem and, even if the request itself didn't really come from the men's mother, it may reflect a memory that this woman was part of the wider group.

Curiously, Matthew is not the only Gospel to erase Salome's name. She does not appear in any list of women in either Luke or John. In John 19:25 the women at the cross of Jesus were 'his mother, and his mother's sister, Mary the wife of Clopas, and Mary Magdalene'. Because of this, it was thought in later times that Salome was also called Mary. A medieval French legend claimed that Jesus' grandmother (St Anne) had three different daughters by three different husbands, each of them named Mary – Mary the mother of Jesus, Mary of Clopas and Mary Salome. It is that conflation that is commemorated now in the Western tradition, with the feast day of Saint 'Mary Salome' on 22 October. But there is actually no good reason to think of her as a Mary.

If we go back to Mark, which is the earliest account, it is striking that Salome is mentioned without any further information, as if readers would automatically know who she was, even though her name was incredibly common. This is similar to how Simon of Cyrene is introduced as the 'father of Alexander and Rufus' (Mark 15:21), as if everyone knew who Alexander and Rufus were too. After witnessing Jesus' death on the cross, Salome appears to be one of the women who witnessed the empty tomb (16:1), going there to anoint Jesus' dead body with *aromata* (perfumed oils) with Mary Magdalene and Mary the mother of James. Salome is just Salome, though, unrelated to anyone.

But here we have to stop and observe that Mark does not write perfectly clearly about Salome. At the cross, she is noted distinctly after the other two Marys (15:40). In 15:47, however, Mark mentions only the two Marys, watching and seeing where Jesus was laid. After this, we learn that when the Sabbath was over (at sundown) 'Mary Magdalene and Mary the (mother) of James and Salome bought *aromata*' and came to the tomb (16:1–2). All together, in this final mention it can be read as if the second Mary is actually the mother of James, Joses *and Salome*, and that there were only two women who went to the tomb, which is what Matthew opts for in his version of the story (28:1): Mary Magdalene and the other Mary went there together. This other Mary is often identified with Mary the Mother, since Jesus' brothers are listed indeed as '*James, Joses*, Judas and Simon', along with some (unnamed) sisters as well (Mark 6:3).

If Salome was not at the tomb, Mary the Mother being described as the mother of James *and Salome* is itself an indication of her importance: mothers are usually identified by sons, not daughters. If she was at the tomb, she is mentioned again by name as someone everyone knew. Whichever way we look at it, just being Salome was enough to distinguish her for the Gospel's audience. If she was the sister of Jesus, she was also a disciple whom people remembered well.

We can see her memory continuing into the second century. Mary Magdalene and Salome appear together as the two foremost female disciples of Jesus in a couple of early Gospels that did not get included in the New Testament: the *Gospel of Thomas* and the *Gospel of the Egyptians*. The *Gospel of Thomas* is a series of sayings of Jesus, without context. It is quite bald and there is no introduction to anyone, but it may well contain some reliable memories of the disciples. Male and female disciples asked Jesus questions, and Jesus answered. Here, Salome hosted Jesus for dinner (61), as she said of Jesus, 'You have climbed up on my couch and eaten from my table.' This suggests she was remembered as an independent woman with her own couch and table.

The *Gospel of the Egyptians* is known only from snippets quoted by early Christian scholars. In one, Salome asked Jesus a question: 'How long will death rule?'

He replied, 'So long as you women have children.'

She said, 'Well, I've done the right thing in not giving birth.'

This seems to preserve another memory about her: she was childless. She did not say here that she had remained unmarried, only that she had not had children, and Jesus actually endorsed her for this. This is remarkable because, in the social world of the time, a woman's status and security often depended on her being a mother, ideally a mother of many children. If we think about the term 'prostitute' (*pornē, zonah*) as sometimes applying to a woman who was 'barren', resulting in divorce and social stigma, then perhaps that gives us a real clue about her. Truly, Salome is not the mother or wife of anyone.

Salome is also mentioned along with other female disciples (Mary, Martha and an unknown woman named Arsinoe) in a passing comment in another second-century text called *The (First) Apocalypse of James*, again as if everyone would know who she was. She's mentioned among female disciples of Jesus in diverse literature of different early Christian traditions. She is recorded in a Gospel synthesis, the *Diatessaron*, by Tatian (*c.*180 CE) as being quite distinct from the mother of the sons of Zebedee. Around the same time, the anti-Christian philosopher Celsus identified Salome as the founder of a distinctive Christian group (see text box, 'The problem with women', p. 17). All this collectively gives us the impression that she was well remembered by successive generations of Christians, and known as a disciple and teacher.

We get a rather different version, however, in a slightly odd work known as the *Secret Gospel of Mark*, a version of the Gospel used by some in Alexandria in the second century. Here, Salome is marginalised, as this Gospel reads (at Mark 10:46), 'Then he came into Jericho. And the sister of the young man whom Jesus loved was there with his mother and Salome, but Jesus would not receive them.' This harks back to the incident where the mother of Jesus came to Jesus in Capernaum, along with his brothers and sisters, and stood outside his house asking for him (Mark 3:31–35). It was this that prompted Jesus to announce that all those who do the will of God are his mother, brothers and sisters. The writer of this amendment to Mark seems to remember Salome as Jesus' sister, but then presents her as being spurned, along with the sister of 'the disciple Jesus loved' and Jesus' mother, as if to say that this is the right attitude towards her and the other women. Keep your distance!

Elsewhere, as with all the female disciples of Jesus, Salome's story morphed in various ways. There was also an alternative

Salome. In the *Protevangelium of James* (19–20), another text from the second or third century, Salome was still associated with Mary the Mother, possibly still as Jesus' sister; she was outside the Bethlehem cave where Jesus was born, and initially doubted the testimony of Mary's midwife that Mary was a virgin. She put her finger in Mary's vagina to examine her, and was duly punished with a painful hand, at which point she begged God to restore her, asking, 'Give me to the poor. For you know, Master, that I have done service in your name and received my wages from you.'

There's clearly a backstory to this Salome, who had worked in divine service, and was told not to 'report all the miraculous actions you have seen until the child enters Jerusalem', which implied a further role for her in the holy city, but this simply points to a missing story of this Salome we will never know. However, later on, in the seventh- to eighth-century *Gospel of Pseudo-Matthew*, Salome became the midwife. In another late text, the *History of Joseph the Carpenter*, she accompanied the holy family to Egypt as a midwife/nurse. Indeed, the strand of thinking that has her unrelated to Jesus is found already in the fourth-century *Apostolic Constitutions* (3:6).

We only have tiny vestiges in the surviving literature that might help us think more about the real Salome. But if we take these memories seriously, she was Jesus' sister (or half-sister), who was either unmarried or widowed or divorced, childless, and then an independent disciple of Jesus who became a teacher in her own right, with her own following. There's no good reason to separate out these roles as indicating different women, one who was the sister of Jesus and another who was the disciple and teacher. She was part of the wider blood family of Jesus that included James, identified by Paul as an apostle (Gal. 1:19; 1 Cor. 15:7), who came to lead the Jerusalem Church and who was himself killed by the authorities.

The siblings of Jesus were highly esteemed by the earliest Jewish disciples of Jesus, and known to Paul, who was mainly engaged with the male 'brothers' (1 Cor. 9:5). When the term *adelphoi* appears in Greek, though, it's important to remember that it can include sisters too. So in John (7:3, 10) we could read that the *adelphoi*, 'brothers and sisters', of Jesus encouraged him to go to Judaea to a festival in Jerusalem. In Acts 1:13 they were with Mary the Mother in the Upper Room. We need to imagine Salome in such scenes.

We can also reach back before Jesus' mission begins, to imagine Salome growing up with Jesus' other siblings in Nazareth, as part of the family of the carpenter Joseph, living in a small, simple village in the heart of the densely populated region of Galilee. The village was embedded in wine country, where wealthy estate owners hired day labourers to tend the vines, and it lay close to a stone vessel manufacturing industry. Nothing suggests that the family was wealthy. Salome's brothers would have been trained in the trade of their father, but she would have been trained in all the work of *diakonia* fitting for a wife and mother, providing for the needs of the wider family: grinding grain, fetching water, preparing and serving food, spinning, weaving, laundering, sewing, growing vegetables, cleaning, caring for children and the elderly, and looking after the health of the family with knowledge of remedies and amulets.

Jesus observed her and the other women of the household closely, learning such important female lessons as not sewing on new, unshrunk cloth to patch old garments (Matt. 9:16). If Salome married, she would have been between twelve and sixteen at the time, and would have gone to live with her husband's extended family. Yet in a small village this would not have been far from home.

At some point Jesus left Nazareth and returned as a prophet, and the family had to deal with terrible controversy about what Jesus was up to, even trying to restrain him (Mark 3:20–21). By this time Salome would have been on her own, supporting her (widowed?) mother, initially trying to talk sense to her brother and call him back from his apparent 'new family' in Capernaum. Salome's journey from confusion to acceptance must have been momentous.

Amazingly, testimony to the memory of a venerated woman named Salome has now been found outside the literary tradition. In 1982, a mysterious cave came to light in excavations near ancient Maresha, in the south-west of Israel, at a site named Horvat Qasra. It is actually an underground chapel built out of a Jewish rock-cut burial cave, and dates from the early Roman period. This cave, where the charcoal of ancient candles still adheres to the walls, is covered in graffiti in Greek, Syriac and Arabic, testifying to a long veneration of a 'holy/Saint Salome', at the 'Shrine of Salome'. In the dark space of this cave there are appeals to Salome for healing, asking her to 'have mercy' on people who honoured her. People came for centuries to remember Salome and appeal to her.

Not recorded anywhere in extant literature, the underground chapel dates perhaps from the third century to at least the seventh. Whatever the case, it is a poignant example of how ancient memories and traditions relating to Jesus' female disciples have been lost over the course of time, and we can only imagine what stories were told.

The excavators of this chapel associated the Salome venerated here with the late textual evidence of Mother Mary's midwife companion, but from the graffiti we can see that Salome was prayed to specifically. It was common for people to appeal to saints in this way, for help and healing, and to leave graffiti scratched on the wall with their appeals, but the midwife Salome was never a saint. Was this Salome, then, Jesus' disciple and sister?

3

Joanna (and Susanna)

Joanna is known only from the Gospel of Luke, where she is mentioned twice, along with some fascinating details that suggest she was of rather higher status than most of the other women. Strangely, despite her connections with the Herodian court and impressive-sounding husband, Joanna has never captured popular attention. She hardly gets a mention in early Christian literature, though today she is honoured as a saint and has recently enjoyed a speaking role in two TV mini-series from 2015 (*Killing Jesus* and *A.D.: The Bible Continues*) And although she is well known in scholarly circles, the full implications of what Luke has to say about her have largely been overlooked in popular culture.

As with Salome, analysis of a woman who appears in only one Gospel source is always potentially problematic, and it's as well to confront the difficulty head on from the start. Luke has it that she was married to Herod's steward (*epitropos*) and that she and others ministered, served or provided for Jesus and the twelve male disciples out of their own resources (Luke 8:3). The clear implication is that she was a wealthy woman of some status.

What makes the description problematic is the fact that the author of Luke was very keen to suggest that the Christian movement attracted the well-to-do, especially well-to-do women (we might think of Lydia in Acts 16:11–15 or the leading women of Athens in Acts 17:4). The reason for this is quite easy to detect: we've already seen that one of the criticisms levelled against early Christianity was that it attracted common women (of doubtful reputation) and beggars, the implication being that no decent people would join such a movement. An easy way to counter this was for the author of Luke to stress that Christianity appealed to respectable people, even people of wealth and status (Paul the Roman citizen, Titius Justus in Acts 18, and so on). Where women in particular are mentioned, they tended to be rich and/or aristocratic. But what are we to make of this? Are we to conclude that these women were nothing more than Lukan creations?

Perhaps not. Luke 8:2–3 is a reworking of Mark's comment in 15:40–41 that many women had followed Jesus from Galilee, but there is no reason to suppose that it doesn't contain authentic memories that have been woven in. In Mark, three women are singled out – perhaps because they are known to the author's particular audience – and in Luke three different women are listed (only Mary Magdalene appears in both lists). Given that there are 'many women' in Jesus' entourage, the author of Luke could presumably have singled out whichever women the audience knew; if Joanna was well known to the congregation, it would make sense to note her presence here. It certainly suits the themes of the Gospel to stress her connections and wealth, but there is no reason to doubt them completely.

If we place the two representations of the women disciples of Jesus side by side, we can see quite precisely where alternative material has been woven into the Markan fabric, with specific substitutions. Luke 8:1 actually picks up on wording found in a common source also used in Matthew (4:23; 9:35), but there is more in Luke than in Matthew. The hook for including Mark's material is the mention of women.

Mark 15	Luke 8
[40] There were also **women** looking on from a distance; among whom were also **Mary Magdalene** and Mary the mother of James the Younger and Joses, and Salome.[41] They used to follow him and minister to him when he was in Galilee; and there were **many other women** who had come up with him to Jerusalem.	and the Twelve were with him [2] and certain **women** who were cured of evil spirits and infirmities, Mary called the Magdalene, from whom seven demons were expelled, [3] and Joanna wife of Chuza, steward of Herod, and Susanna and **many others**, who **ministered/provided for** them (or: **him**) out of their resources.

Notice that in the brackets there is an alternative reading of Luke 8:3, whereby the women 'ministered to *him*', in line with Mark. That's the sort of thing that creeps into manuscripts when copyists know one Gospel and think another Gospel should say the same thing: it is called harmonisation, and it's common in our texts. So it is more likely that Luke read 'them'. This is important, because it ties in with what we've seen about female companions of the male envoys of Jesus, or the 'sister wives' Paul held up as customary. It seems as if here some of them are being named specifically.

So why mention Chuza's position? The author of Luke–Acts takes a particular interest in the Herods and mentions them and people connected with the court more than any other evangelist. This may be part of a strategy to raise the standing of the earliest Christ-followers, but more likely use was made of a source, perhaps a body of oral memories that derived from Herod's court. Perhaps such memories may even have come down to the congregation through Joanna herself. In any case, these recollections are a valuable reminder that, despite its popularity in the rural villages of Galilee, the Christian message reached the highest levels of the urban elite relatively quickly. And while Herod Antipas himself had nothing but scorn for the new faith, there were those at court who found it attractive.

In Luke, the decision to introduce Jesus' women disciples early on subtly changes the whole tenor of Jesus' ministry; 8:1–3 is actually a highly significant passage for our study. The author describes Jesus' itinerant ministry as he made his way through the 'cities and villages' of Galilee, preaching and bringing the good news of the kingdom of God (v.1). Next, it is noted that the Twelve were with Jesus (they had already been chosen and named in 6:13–16), along with 'certain women who had been cured of evil spirits and infirmities' – including Mary Magdalene, Joanna and Susanna. All indications are that the women had exactly the same relationship with Jesus as the twelve male envoys, that they had also been with Jesus from his earliest ministry and that they would play an equal part in proclaiming the kingdom of God. All that sets them apart is the fact that they provided for/ministered to the group from their own resources – something we'll come back to.

For Luke, then, women were an integral and equal part of Jesus' mission from the start. But how did Joanna end up as part of this group? And, more intriguingly, how did she end up on the road with Jesus?

A good marriage

Any discussion of Joanna has to start with her mysterious husband. Chuza is a Nabataean name, suggesting that he came from the large Arabian kingdom to the south-east and east of Judaea. The Herods had enjoyed close connections with Nabataea for more than a century: Herod the Great's mother was an Arab, and Herod Antipas' first wife was the daughter of Aretas IV of Nabataea. Both of these women would have arrived with their own entourage of courtiers and advisors, and we might well expect that the two courts were in close contact. Chuza may have come on his own, or perhaps he was the son of courtiers. Most probably he converted to Judaism: as a Nabataean he would already have been circumcised, and the chances of promotion at Antipas' court would doubtlessly have been enhanced if he were to take on the prevailing religion (even if Antipas himself was hardly a paragon of piety).

Chuza is described as Antipas' *epitropos*, a Greek term that means a manager, guardian or steward. The word is used in Jesus' parable of the labourers in the vineyard (Matt. 20:1–16), where it's the duty of the *epitropos* to pay the hired men at the end of the day. The historian Josephus describes another *epitropos* of a Herodian king whose duty it was to convey royal goods. Named Ptolemaios (an Egyptian name), he served Agrippa II in leading a convoy of expensive clothes, silver and gold (*Life* 127). Herod Antipas' *epitropos* would doubtless have been an important and trusted administrator, perhaps the equivalent of a finance minister or the manager of his extensive estates. Such a man would have been a high-ranking official at court, a person of wealth and status, perhaps owning land himself.

What, then, of Joanna? She bore a popular Jewish name and might well have come from a noble and wealthy Galilean family, perhaps with estates of their own. In regard to political sympathies they must have been pro-Herod. Perhaps they hoped that Herod Antipas would one day exchange the lesser title of tetrarch (literally ruler of a quarter territory) for that of king, and that he would rule over an extended land of Israel as his father Herod the Great once had.

Joanna and Chuza made their home in the newly built city of Tiberias, on the western shore of the Sea of Galilee. The city had been founded around 18–20 CE by Antipas to serve as his main residence and new administrative capital in the region. Like his father before him, Antipas aspired to be a great builder; he had already rebuilt the city of Sepphoris, which was only a little more than an hour's walk from Nazareth. Now he spared no expense as he set about constructing a second city in the narrow stretch of land between the lake shore and the hills beyond. The site's proximity to natural hot springs at the small settlement of Emmaus to the south added to its attractions. Antipas gave it all the trappings of a Roman city: a beautiful monumental gate led into the city from the south, after which a visitor would find an agora (or marketplace), council buildings, a stadium, a theatre, a quay along the shoreline to accommodate trade across the lake and possibly hot baths (though these may have been from a later period). Buildings were made from the local black basalt, which sparkled in the sun, or were covered in white plaster. And high up on the hillside he built a splendid palace, with golden ceilings and ornate decorations, from where he and his court could see and be seen all across the lake.

There would have been a strong element of competition with the thriving urban centres on the east of the lake, especially Hippos and Gadara (both part of the Decapolis, or ten cities, belonging to Syria). Antipas would not have wanted his own cities to be any less impressive than those across the water, whose lights would have been visible as night descended on the lake. The end result was a remarkable monument to Herodian power in the region, with the city giving its name to the lake, now often known as the Sea of Tiberias.

Josephus told a very odd story about the founding of the city, which has had a profound effect on the way it has been remembered. He claims that an old cemetery was disturbed in the course of the building works. This would have made the inhabitants ritually unclean because of corpse impurity, and so in a desperate bid to populate his new city Antipas was reduced to moving soldiers, non-Jews and slaves there by force or bribery (*Antiquities* 18:38). Variations on the story appear in later rabbinic texts too, suggesting that there is something behind it.

Flavius Josephus

Much of our detailed knowledge of Roman Palestine comes from the Jewish historian Flavius Josephus. Born in 37 CE to a family of Jerusalem priestly aristocrats, Josephus served as a general in the Jewish war with Rome (66–70 CE) before being taken prisoner, defecting to Rome and ending his days as a writer in the Emperor Vespasian's former residence in Rome.

Despite his dubious war record, Josephus' writings are an invaluable source of information about Judaea and Galilee in the first century. Two are of particular importance. The Jewish War *(written around 75 CE) is an account of the events that led to the outbreak of war with Rome, the course of the war itself and its aftermath. The* Antiquities of the Jews *(written around 93 CE) is an account of Jewish history from creation to the reign of Nero in the 60s, up to when his War begins properly.*

Like all writers, Josephus had his own interests and concerns (not least to defend his own actions), and he paid very little attention to women. But even so, his works provide us with an unparalleled insight into life in Galilee and Judaea in the first century.

What's strange, though, is that the obvious way to deal with a former burial site would be simply to remove it, which would easily have taken away any potential impurity. There was no reason why a former graveyard should continue to pollute a later city once the bones had been relocated elsewhere. In any case, corpse impurity would have been a perennial problem in a society with a high mortality rate, and only the more pietistic groups (such as the Pharisees) or priests would have been particularly worried by it, and most of them lived in Judaea. Most likely the slur reflects tensions between Tiberias and other Galilean cities – most notably Sepphoris, which had found its status considerably diminished with the building of a new capital. Josephus himself had little reason to like the Tiberians – they had refused to join him in the war with Rome – and so he would have had few qualms about passing on such slurs. In fact, there is no evidence for a pagan population in the new city. Quite the reverse: Tiberias could boast a huge synagogue and ritual baths (to remove impurity), and while some of the inhabitants may have been rather lax in their adherence to the Law, there's no reason to think that Tiberias wasn't in essence a Jewish city. Adopting Roman culture and practices didn't necessarily make anyone a bad Jew.

Nor should we overplay any conflict between Antipas' cities and the rural inhabitants of his territories. The population of Galilee grew considerably under Antipas, with many settlers coming up from Judaea in the south to work the fertile land. There was doubtless a degree of urban–rural tension: some would have resented the tax burden of the cities, the strain on food and resources, and the cities' attractiveness to young men who might have been lured there in search of work or brides, and some would have been suspicious of the continual growth of an essentially alien Roman culture in the region. But at the same time, the wealth of a city like Tiberias would have spilled over into the surrounding towns and villages, providing a ready market for local produce such as olives, barley, wine or ceramics. The huge building projects would also have provided a great deal of employment for the surrounding area, requiring both skilled craftsmen and unskilled labourers. And the region as a whole was quiet and stable under Antipas, with no evidence of any major upheavals.

Perhaps the main difference between the city and the neighbouring area was in their attitude to Rome. When the war with Rome broke out in 66 CE, the surrounding region joined the rebels in an effort to throw off the Roman overlords. True to its name, however, Tiberias remained broadly loyal to the Emperor and quickly surrendered to the Roman legions. All of this was several decades in the future, of course, but the pro-Roman sympathies must already have been apparent.

As members of Herod's court, Joanna and Chuza would have lived in a magnificent mansion, most likely with architectural stonework and marble columns, mosaic floors and decorative motifs. Effortlessly taking their place as part of the city's wealthy elite, they would have enjoyed a privileged, luxurious lifestyle far removed from that of most Galilean peasants. When Chuza wasn't busy with Herod's estates and concerns, he and his wife would have mixed with other courtiers, attending dinner parties and enjoying the baths and hot springs. They may well have gone to the splendid theatre – still partly standing today – which faced north so that the sun was behind spectators as they gathered to be entertained.

Joanna probably accompanied the other ladies of Antipas' court to Jerusalem for the feasts, perhaps hoping to catch up with friends and family members while she was there. Did she feel that something was missing from her life? Or was she quite content before she heard about a healer from Nazareth? Luke suggests that she suffered from an illness, though we have no idea what this might have been. At all events, an encounter with Jesus would change her life completely.

Healed by Jesus

We can only guess at how Joanna came across Jesus. No doubt she and the other women at court would have taken a lively interest in Jesus' predecessor, John the Baptist, particularly if he was attracting large crowds. The Gospels suggest that John openly criticised Antipas' marital arrangements (he had divorced his Nabataean wife so that he could marry his half-brother's wife Herodias, who was also his niece – something that was frowned upon in Jewish Law).

John's condemnation would have been the talk of the city, with courtiers openly siding with Antipas (whatever their private views). The tetrarch's execution of John would have been another talking point, with many now taking the view that killing God's prophet was a dubious and even dangerous thing to do. (Some time later, when Antipas was roundly defeated in battle by the King of Nabataea, Josephus tells us that popular opinion held it as God's punishment for his execution of John.) Perhaps all of this encouraged Joanna to think deeply about her life at court and to reflect on John's demand for repentance in the face of impending judgement.

But how would Joanna have met Jesus? There is no evidence that Jesus ever went to Tiberias, or to Antipas' other city Sepphoris. We might well imagine that he would have seemed out of place there – he had given up any path to possessions and status in exchange for a frugal itinerant lifestyle very much at odds with the prevailing city culture. But although he's remembered by the Gospels as being dismissive of those who wore fine clothing and lived in luxury at court (see Luke 7:25, Matt. 11:8), he never condemned the cities – as he did a number of other towns in Luke 10:11–15.

Jesus may have simply preferred the towns and villages of rural Galilee to the cities, though an exchange in Luke may give us some further clues. In Luke 13:31–33, a group of Pharisees warned Jesus that Herod Antipas wanted to kill him. Jesus referred to Antipas as 'that fox', probably a reference to the destructive nature of foxes, and gave the Pharisees a message to take back to him, saying that a prophet can only die in Jerusalem. Maybe Jesus' reluctance to visit the cities was partly because of what had happened to John the Baptist. The cities were very much Antipas' power base, and Jesus couldn't afford to be arrested before he had completed his mission in Jerusalem.

More likely, then, Joanna went out to meet Jesus somewhere, along with crowds of others seeking a cure. It's clear from the Gospels that people often sought out Jesus as he spoke in remote areas. John 6:23 mentions boats from Tiberias taking people across the lake in search of Jesus. If Joanna was among them, she may have been curious to hear him, and particularly drawn to his reputation as a healer. It's sometimes been suggested that the son of the royal official in John 4:46 was Joanna and Chuza's son, though this story is set in Capernaum rather than Tiberias. It's possible that Jesus healed a member of Joanna's family but, given Luke's comment in 8:2, it's more likely that it was she herself who was in need of healing. If so, Jesus not only healed her but also changed her life for ever.

Out on the road

It's clear from Luke that Joanna took to the road with Jesus, the Twelve and other women. What's less clear is Chuza's reaction to all of this. Was he still alive? And if so, was he happy with this arrangement? Was he perhaps a follower too by this time? Jesus' reputation had certainly spread to the court, such that Antipas wondered who he might be, and even speculated on whether he could be John the Baptist raised from the dead. Later on, we hear of another courtier, Manaen, who became a prominent leader of the church in Antioch (Acts 13:1). If Jesus had healed his wife, was Chuza sympathetic to the new movement, despite choosing to remain at his post at court? Or did he reject her? Unfortunately, we can only speculate.

We're on firmer ground when we consider Joanna's role in the Jesus movement. Luke notes that she – along with Mary Magdalene, Susanna and many others – provided for Jesus and the Twelve from their own resources. The word translated 'provided for' here is from the verb *diakoneo*. Although it can denote women's menial household labour and waiting at table, we've already seen that it quickly became associated with ministry in early Christian circles. Presumably the reason for this is because Jesus' whole mission was about putting himself last, shunning the usual status symbols, and being a servant of all. Those who followed him similarly saw themselves as servants of others. In Luke's construction there is an implication that these women were providing for the group financially out of their 'resources'. They were not actually spending their time cooking meals and mending clothing (though someone had to do that), but using their money to benefit the group. Perhaps they bought food from the markets, paid transit tolls when needed, made donations to those who offered hospitality and gave to the poor and needy. Perhaps too they provided for the twelve male apostles' families back home, many of whom would have been struggling financially without the men of the household.

It's clear that the early Christ-followers had a number of different financial models. John mentions a common purse (which these women may have paid into, John 13:29). In the early

Women and wealth

While most work in the home was unpaid, we saw in chapter 1 that there were a variety of ways in which women from the lower social classes might have earned a little money. They could set up a market stall where they might sell farm produce, make bread or clothes, act as midwives or hairdressers, or run an inn. If married, or still living with a father, extra income would have been seen as a contribution to the family and controlled by the husband/father.

Ordinarily, women had independent income only when they were no longer under the authority of a man. Daughters could inherit from their fathers if there were no sons, and we know that fathers often wanted to make provision for their daughters (frequently gifting money or assets to them). Both of these situations are illustrated by Babatha's documents (see box on Polygamy in Chapter 1). Babatha herself inherited her father's property, which included several date palm orchards and seems to have left her comfortably off. Her second husband gifted his first wife's daughter Shelamzion a courtyard, though after his death her teenage brothers contested the gift in court.

Very wealthy women were free to spend their money as they liked, even if it went against the family's position. Josephus tells us that the wife of Herod the Great's younger brother Pheroras was a supporter of the Pharisees. When more than six thousand of them were fined for their refusal to take the oath of allegiance to Herod, this (unnamed) woman paid it for them (Ant 17:41–42).

If a woman was divorced, she would expect to receive a portion of her dowry back (though this may not always have happened), and if she was widowed she might inherit from her husband. Either way, she might either have lived on her own or gone back to live with her family. If the surviving family was only a sister, we could well have the scenario imagined in the Mary and Martha story (see Chapter 6). Thus, while living without a male guardian might be a precarious existence for many women, especially divorcees and widows, those who managed to inherit would have been able to exert a certain amount of autonomy.

chapters of Acts, several disciples sold their possessions and shared the proceeds (Acts 2:44–45; 4:32–5:6), though others held on to them and used them in the service of the church (such as Mary in Acts 12:12–13 who hosted a house church in her home). A woman like Joanna would have had money and influence, both of which would have been of use to the group. She may well have had some level of education, and likely spoke not only Aramaic (the language of the Jewish homeland in this period) but also Greek and perhaps even some Latin. As a woman of status, she would have been used to operating with more freedom, making her a natural leader among the women and a role model for others. Ordinarily, a benefactor would have expected some reward in terms of status and honour from those she sponsored, though again the Jesus movement's countercultural attitude would have made that impossible. Joanna's reward for her patronage wouldn't be public esteem in the present, but entry into God's kingdom in the near future.

Despite their shared devotion to Jesus, there must have been a huge social gulf between someone like Joanna and the fisher-women and others who made up the rest of the group. We can imagine that there would have been at least occasional friction and strain, and that some of the others would have been deeply suspicious of someone with such easy access to powerful circles. Joanna would also have had more to lose in terms of her reputation; it was one thing for working women to join an itinerant group, but an aristocratic woman in their midst would have raised eyebrows. Of course, it's possible that Joanna was related to one of the male disciples, though perhaps unlikely. We might wonder how she thought about associating with a very different group of people. Was she surprised at her own adaptability? Did she see them as a new family, part of the promised kingdom that was growing around Jesus? And did she see herself giving not only her wealth but also her whole life to this new movement?

According to Luke, Jesus appointed seventy disciples (or seventy-two in some translations) to go ahead of him in pairs to every town and village. They were to take nothing with them for the journey (no purse, bag or sandals), and were not to greet anyone on the road. When they came to a town they were to go into a house and stay there, enjoying the hospitality, healing the sick and preaching the kingdom of God. Any town that refused to listen and show hospitality was to be condemned (Luke 10:1–12). Later on, the seventy returned from their mission, reporting great success, particularly in their abilities to cast out evil spirits (Luke 10:17–20). It's almost certain that Joanna and the other women would have been part of this group.

As we saw with the account of Jesus sending out the Twelve 'two by two' (presumably with female partners), we can imagine that a male and a female disciple travelled together and shared ministry in each new town – the woman healing and teaching other women, and the male disciple going to the men. It was a highly gendered world, and divisions between male and female space were common. A female missionary would have found it much easier to seek out the women of a town at the well or the marketplace, to enter into their private gatherings and to win their trust. In these smaller, more intimate settings, Joanna might have healed and anointed others, and perhaps baptised them into the new movement.

This is true also of Susanna, who is found along with Joanna in the list of women in Luke (though not now venerated as a saint). Like Salome, discussed in the previous chapter, she is mentioned simply by her name, as if everyone knew her, and given no association with any man as someone's mother or wife. However, unlike Salome, Susanna was not a common name; in fact, it was quite rare, though Susanna was the heroine of a story found only in the Greek version of the Jewish Scriptures (Dan. 13). Strangely, as with Joanna, she is hardly mentioned at all in early Christian writings, but turns up as the prime woman supporter of Jesus in the writings of the scholar Origen in the third century, defending Jesus against the attacks of Celsus: 'there were certain women who had been healed of their illnesses, among whom was Susanna, who from their own resources provided the disciples the means of support' (*Against Celsus* 1:65). So was Susanna quite a star, then? Was she of the same high status as Joanna? Once again, we can only speculate.

We'll meet Joanna again at the end of our story when Luke puts her with the other women at the cross and the empty tomb. No doubt she was able to make use of her contacts in Jerusalem that last, fateful Passover. If Luke is right to suggest that Pilate sent Jesus to Herod Antipas for some kind of trial or interrogation (Luke 23:6–12), then Joanna would have easily been able to find out what was happening on that confused and dreadful evening. And Joanna was no doubt among 'the eleven and their companions' (Luke 24:33) who heard the testimony of the couple on the road to Emmaus, and who were subsequently commissioned by Jesus to be witnesses of his resurrection.

4

Mary Magdalene

The first-named woman in the lists of female disciples in Mark 15 and Luke 8 is Mary Magdalene. Many people today know of her as the woman closest to Jesus. Indeed, she is far more attested in the Gospels and in early Christian literature than any of the other women, apart from Jesus' mother. Many books have been written about her. She's so famous she even has her own fictionalised biopic, in the form of the movie *Mary Magdalene*, directed by Garth Davis (2018).

People sometimes like to imagine her as being in a (potential or realised) sexual relationship with Jesus. Dan Brown's bestselling novel *The Da Vinci Code* made her into the wife of Jesus and matriarch of a royal European bloodline. She's portrayed in the video for Lady Gaga's song 'Judas' as torn between her love for Jesus and his betrayer, Judas. In the film of *Jesus Christ Superstar* (1973) she sings, 'I don't know how to love him', regarding Jesus with all the strong emotion of a yearning woman whose feelings are not reciprocated.

More conventionally, Mary Magdalene is frequently presented as a repentant prostitute. This is the kind of Mary we have in *The Last Temptation of Christ*, directed by Martin Scorsese (1988), in which Mary is the woman caught in adultery (John 8:2–11) whom Jesus defends by challenging those who would accuse her, asking the one without sin to 'cast the first stone'. In the film, based on the book by Nikos Kazantzakis, Mary is a reformed sex worker, a beautiful woman who made her living from her body. But the love interest element is there in this work too.

From the very earliest filmic portrayals, 'sexy Mary' is stamped onto the minds of filmgoers. In Cecil B. DeMille's fantastically successful and deeply sentimental film *The King of Kings* (1927), a scantily clad Mary enjoys herself with her suitors as a wealthy courtesan. She snuggles with her pet leopard and gets around in a chariot pulled by zebras. The lush orientalism of the depiction creates an erotic, self-aggrandising aura around Mary that utterly contrasts with the depiction of the saintly, pious Mary the Mother. Mary Magdalene is tamed by the eviction of seven demons, shown as the seven deadly sins, at which point she passes from autonomous waywardness to controlled devotion to her man, Christ.

Such portrayals of Mary Magdalene were completely to be expected. The Western Church had long identified Mary Magdalene as the unnamed repentant 'sinner' of Luke 7:36–50, who burst into a dinner scene in Galilee, wept at Jesus' feet, kissed and anointed those feet with ointment and wiped them with her loose hair. Interestingly, the Eastern Church ended up making no such equation: Mary Magdalene was simply the leading 'myrrh-bearing woman' on Easter morning, pious and modest, and the most important of Jesus' female disciples.

UNTRUE

Remembering Mary Magdalene

But how was she first remembered? Of all Jesus' female disciples, it is Mary Magdalene who is the most frequently mentioned in the Gospels. She appears in all the accounts of the women at the crucifixion and at the empty tomb. In two accounts, she is the first person who witnesses the resurrected Jesus (Mark 16:9–10; John 20:11–18), and in one she is accompanied by the 'other Mary' (Matt. 28:1–10).

This may seem to us to guarantee her importance. However, as we've seen, the crucial role of women in the proclamation of the Church was not appreciated as a positive in the patriarchal society of the ancient world. At the beginning of our study, we noted the very negative statements made by various critics of Christianity when it came to the leadership of women. In the mid-second century, Celsus dismissed the earliest testimony to Jesus' resurrection as coming from 'a delirious woman' (Origen, *Against Celsus* 2:55). Yet even Celsus noted in passing that Mariamme and Martha were Christian women who had a following, so much so that there were people who identified with them by name – as Mariammians or Marthans (5:62). In the Gospels, Mary's name is found either in its Greek form (Maria) or in Aramaic (Mariam), but in Christian texts outside the New Testament, Mary Magdalene's name can be found also as Mariamme or Mariamne. Does this comment by Celsus testify to a group who claimed to follow Mary Magdalene as their teacher and founder?

Evidence for such a group was discovered at the end of the nineteenth century in the form of a part of a lost Gospel, known as the *Gospel of Mary*. The place of its discovery was Akhmim, in Egypt, the site of a town named Panopolis, where tombs had been robbed and their contents offered on the antiquities market. This Gospel was in an ancient book, written in Coptic, that contained other apocryphal works. These testify to the *Gospel of Mary*'s use in a community focused on mystical revelation, often termed 'Gnostic' (*gnosis* means 'knowledge' in Greek).

Later on, further fragments of the same work came to light, this time in Greek. The Gospel's precise meaning and identification are much debated. What is clear, though, is that Mary is the leading figure. The scene we find in one fragment opens with Mary and the male apostles gathering after Jesus' death. She comforts the apostles, who are afraid of the authorities, and reveals to them visions of what Jesus has shown to her. At the end of this, Peter scoffs that Jesus would not have spoken like this to a woman, and she recoils, hurt that he does not trust her and is accusing her of making things up. Other apostles come to her defence, but this scene suggests that those who claim to follow Mary have been painfully marginalised by those who claim to follow Peter.

Also found in Akhmim, around the same time, was another second-century Gospel, known as the *Gospel of Peter*. In this case there is nothing particularly 'Gnostic' about it. Here, Mary is definitively called a 'disciple' (Greek: *mathetria*), not just someone who happened to trail along with Jesus. Interestingly too, after Jesus' burial in the tomb is described, she is introduced as one

Apocryphal Gospels

The women disciples of Jesus are mentioned a number of times in Gospels dating from the early second century that weren't included in the New Testament. Some of these are mainstream, and some are not. Most we know only from fragments, as they didn't get copied down through the centuries. They are now dubbed 'apocryphal' (literally meaning 'taken out of the cupboard') rather than 'canonical' (meaning 'according to rule'). In ancient times, different groups had them well and truly out of the cupboard and read alongside or instead of the Gospels we have in our New Testament.

Scholars distinguish different types of thinking in these Gospels, and try to link them with known groups, but this is not always possible. One grouping of such Gospels is defined as 'Gnostic'. In Greek, gnosis means 'knowledge', and there were varieties of early Christians who considered that Christian salvation was brought about by the knowledge Jesus brought about the nature of the soul and the universe, and how to attain release from the world. The Gospel of Thomas and the Gospel of Philip, for example, are placed in this category. They turned up in an extraordinarily well-preserved collection of Gnostic writings found in Nag Hammadi, Egypt, in 1945. Other Gospels are harder to define: the Gospel of Mary is sometimes thought of as Gnostic, and sometimes not. The Gospel of Peter is theologically mainstream overall, but just didn't make the final cut.

'who had not done at the tomb of the Lord what the women customarily do for those loved ones who die'. Taking with her some friends, she went to the tomb, stooped down, received a message from a young man in white clothing, and fled, too afraid to tell the other disciples what she and her friends had seen.

Here there is an emphasis on the vital testimony being that of the men, not really of the women. The *Gospel of Peter* reserves the really important resurrection sequence for Peter (the first-person narrator) and other male apostles. After mourning through to the end of the Feast, the men went back home to Galilee. Our text breaks off just as Peter and Andrew went fishing, taking with them Levi son of Alphaeus and probably others, but the narrative clearly originally contained a story of a resurrection appearance to them, perhaps one similar to John 21:1–14, by the lake.

With versions such as this that marginalised Mary's role in the resurrection story, we need to ask why there were ever stories of women witnessing the risen Jesus. Assuming the women disciples were needed simply to witness to the facts that Jesus truly died and was buried, and that the (same) tomb was found empty on the Sunday morning, why not just leave it at that? Why was there ever anything else?

Perhaps it has something to do with the special relationship between Mary and Jesus. The *Gospel of Peter* properly calls Mary a 'disciple' and identifies her as someone with the sole responsibility of doing what female relatives of the much-loved deceased person were supposed to do at the tomb. That in itself spells out what the other Gospels do not say: Mary, of all female disciples and Jesus' own relatives, had a relationship with Jesus that made it *her* responsibility to bring other women as her companions. It was her *job* to bury Jesus: she was the closest woman to him in his new family of disciples.

It is this lovingness and special relationship between Jesus and Mary Magdalene that is found reflected in second-century Gnostic texts, most especially the *Gospel of Philip*, found also in Egypt, in 1945, in a place called Nag Hammadi, near an ancient town named Chenoboskion. In this text the male disciples were jealous of the relationship between Jesus and Mary. They didn't understand why he loved her so much and kissed her like he did. They wished they had the same connection.

In such second-century texts, then, there is a general sense that Mary Magdalene's memory was awkward, and this alerts us to the subtle turns of the canonical Gospels themselves. Testimony from a 'delirious woman' just did not look that great. It provided a reason for the Gospel writers to hide the women, and perhaps especially Mary.

Mary in the Gospels

If we take a memory approach to our texts, rather than attempt-
ing to isolate the earliest textual layer (which is how scholars
usually work), we can cluster elements of the story into certain
'memory' groups, stretching between our Gospels and the early
Christian texts outside the Bible. We have a number of resurrection accounts, all stemming from the first and second centuries,
and we can group them. In the first group we see the evidence for
what is implied in the *Gospel of Mary*: a marginalisation of Mary's
testimony to her encounter with Christ.

In the Gospel of Mark, the oldest Gospel, Mary Magdalene is
suddenly introduced when she was watching Jesus' crucifixion
from a distance with other women who had come up with Jesus
to Jerusalem (15:40–41), as we saw. Mary Magdalene heads the
list, as if she was the most pre-eminent of all the female disciples
and everyone would know her. But she is a missing person in the
previous pages of Jesus' story.

Moving Mary and the other women further back to Galilee, to
make them visible, is what we find in Luke, as we saw in the
previous chapter on Joanna. They were right there in Jesus'
mission in Galilee, on the road with him and the Twelve. Here
Mary also heads the list, but now she is defined as someone who
had been cured, like the other women, in that seven demons had
gone out of her. In Jewish folk medicine of this time, demons
were what caused illness, physical and mental. She's someone
who, like the other women, provided for Jesus/the Twelve 'out of
their resources', whatever they may have been, great or small,
after they had been healed. On the road with Jesus and the Twelve
named men, they were part of his team, engaged in the work.

As for events at the tomb, there are different story elements
that appear in different Gospels, and these can be clustered
together. The first one to note is the element of not believing a
woman's testimony. The Gospel of Mark itself has two different
endings attested in our most ancient manuscripts, what we call
the short ending and the longer ending. In the longer ending of
the Gospel of Mark (16:9–20) and in the Gospel of Luke (24), the

male disciples simply did not believe Mary (that she had seen Jesus in Mark) or the women who returned from the empty tomb (in Luke): 'but these words seemed an idle tale, and they did not believe them' (Luke 24:11). The Gospel of John has Simon Peter and another disciple running to the tomb after Mary announced it was empty, and it was only then that they 'believed' (20:8). That Mary was remembered as not being trusted by the men indicates knowledge that there was an issue about women's testimony, and it continued to affect those who claimed Mary as their guiding light, as we see similarly in the *Gospel of Mary*.

We also have stories in which the risen Jesus only appeared to a group of men, not to any women at all. In the short ending of the Gospel of Mark (16:1–8), we have something actually very similar to the *Gospel of Peter*: Mary and her companion, Mary the mother of James, and Salome, saw where Jesus was laid, and went to anoint him on the third day. They found the empty tomb and were directed by the young man inside it to tell the disciples to go to Galilee where they would see Jesus. But they ran away and said nothing to anyone because they were afraid. They did not see Jesus, and that is it. Unlike in the *Gospel of Peter*, though, there's not even a resurrection scene with the men. It is a curious version because the story of them not telling the male disciples paradoxically also contains the opposite message: for the story to be recorded, they must have informed *someone*.

In Luke 24, the women witnessed the empty tomb and the announcement by the two angels there, and told the unbelieving men; then Jesus arrived in a room with the men and asked them to touch him, and ate fish with them. So these three Gospel accounts all go for a model of women witnesses to the empty tomb but male witnesses to the risen Christ. *Mt 28:9-10*

It is quite likely that different versions of the story were told very early on. In 1 Corinthians 15:3–8, Paul tells of resurrection appearances to men that do not mention Mary Magdalene or the women. There are several other second-century Christian texts that describe how the risen Christ came to 'those with Peter', not to the women, for example in a letter of Ignatius (*Smyrnians* 3), the *Gospel of the Hebrews* and the *Doctrine of Peter*, which evens says 'Take hold, handle me, and see that I am not a bodiless daemon', in terms perfectly unsuited to any form of Jewish concept at the time ('bodiless daemon' evoking highly Greek ways of thinking). But this version of the story ticked all the right boxes: Jesus showed himself to trustworthy men who actually touched him. No delirious woman seeing visions here!

Hermeneutic of suspicion

To read with a hermeneutic of suspicion is very important in feminist method, especially as defined by the great theorist Elisabeth Schüssler Fiorenza. 'Hermeneutics' is the science of interpretation. Everything we read is interpreted by us in some way, either unconsciously or consciously. To read stories about women with a hermeneutic of suspicion means we are suspicious about why women are presented in a certain way, given the patriarchal and hierarchical societal norms of the time. We have to be alert to the rhetorical programme of the writer, in which women and other socially non-esteemed people may always be shown as marginal. In any given story we have to ask what is being emphasised, and what is being hidden?

Because of the kinds of criticisms that could ensue, or because of the debates in communities about the roles of women, female characters could be presented in ways that 'put them in their place', to make them safe and respectable. They could be shown in stereotypical ways, either as vain queens or docile housekeepers. They could be used as examples of virtue or vice. They could be silenced, so that only male characters have speaking roles. We need to ask: why is this woman presented like this? Are there slippages that indicate that we're not being told the whole story?

Approaching a text with a hermeneutic of suspicion is one stage in the process of interpretation, and we may answer by trusting the presentation, on the whole, but we should make sure to take a moment to think before we go on.

It's for this reason that we need to return to our earlier question of why there was ever an alternative version that has Mary Magdalene witnessing the risen Jesus alone. We may be pleased that such stories have survived in our Gospels, but we need to read them with a 'hermeneutic of suspicion' in terms of how Mary is presented, because we know the issues of how a 'delirious woman' could be viewed.

In the longer ending of Mark (16:9–13), which is often considered less original than the short ending noted above, we find that Mary did not run away afraid; whatever happened, she was still there, by the tomb, but now alone. Jesus simply 'appeared' to her, and yet it is said here that she was one from whom Jesus had cast out seven demons. Including that particular piece of information at this very point (rather than earlier, when she is first mentioned) is strange. Surely this is designed to defend Mary and to stress her validity at this crucial time. Earlier on, Jesus' own statements and healing actions were dismissed by people who thought he had a demon (Mark 3:22). But here the demons had been expelled: Mary was no longer subject to them. No one can say she was mentally deranged then. She was in her right mind.

In Matthew (28:1–10) the story is similar. Mary Magdalene was not introduced until the crucifixion scene, where everything was slightly more developed in various directions. Only two women (Mary and the other Mary) went to the tomb. Neither of them ran away afraid. After meeting an angel in the empty tomb, they went off to tell 'the disciples', who in Matthew are generally narrowed down to only the Twelve (named men) envoys. As with the longer ending of Mark, Jesus appeared, but here he said hello, and then the women touched his feet (so we learn he was not an apparition) and venerated him in some way. The duplication of women diffuses any focus on Mary Magdalene's testimony alone, and thus develops a previously known single appearance story.

In John, Mary Magdalene saw Jesus on her own, but we need to see how she is presented holistically. As with Mark and Matthew, she is not introduced specifically by name until the cross. Here she was no longer standing at a distance, and her companions are now identified as 'his mother and his mother's sister, Mary the wife of Clopas and Mary Magdalene' (John 19:25–27), prompting many a discussion about whether there were two, three or four different women. The *Gospel of Philip* remembers these as being three, all called Mary, and that is probably the most likely reading, but here Mary Magdalene is mentioned last. Why last? What is this Gospel concerned about?

The matter is complicated by the reference to 'seeing then his mother and *the disciple Jesus loved* standing near her, Jesus said to his mother, "Woman, this is your son." Then he turned to the disciple and said, "This is your mother"' (John 19:25–26). Since the 'disciple' here is given in masculine terms, John clearly meant to differentiate Mary Magdalene from the disciple Jesus loved, but there is enough ambiguity preserved to make people wonder – especially given that the disciple seemed to pop up from nowhere with the women.

The fact that in the Gospel of John Mary is placed last in the list of women and only turns up at this point leaves us with the impression that the Gospel is not entirely Mary-friendly, and has defence strategies in mind – even though it preserves by far the longest and most detailed account of Mary alone meeting the risen Christ. But even in this story she was in the end in a lesser place than the men.

John (20:14–18) tells a story of a lone Mary Magdalene seeing Jesus, as in the longer ending of the Gospel of Mark. There are Lukan elements here also, but in John there is the fullest extant description of Mary's encounter with Jesus. She thought he was the gardener, and asked where he had put the body of Jesus, given that the tomb was empty. Jesus said, 'Mary,' and she responded, in Hebrew, 'Rabbouni!' While in John it is said that this means 'Teacher', in fact, it means 'my Great One', an entirely appropriate way of addressing one's teacher, which demonstrates that she was a disciple. But she did not touch Jesus. In fact, he specifically told her, 'Don't touch me.' She didn't get that important hands-on verification, a hug or a kiss, and touching was reserved for the men, specifically doubting Thomas (John 20:24–29) and the others who had a fish breakfast with Jesus by the lake shore (John 21:1–19).

In our Gospels, then, Mary Magdalene is positioned at the heart of the Christian proclamation of Christ's livingness, but there are several different memories preserved about her involvement, and various defence strategies, from omission to mitigation.

A literary approach would simply try to work out which Gospel story was the oldest one and trace its influence, but in the case of the 'who saw Jesus first?' mystery, which was so important to the proclamation of the Church, we have a much more complex situation, whereby later literary stories may preserve earlier tellings, and earlier ones erase them. Along with what we have preserved in literature, it is likely that there were others not preserved, and oral tellings as well.

Laura James, The Holy Women at the Sepulchre *(2000)*

The mystery of what really happened at the tomb may be answered in different ways. What role did Mary Magdalene really play? When we think of these stories as being told in different places, and with specific defensive strategies in mind, perhaps we should best ask, which one is least defensive when it comes to the 'delirious' woman of anti-Christian rhetoric?

Magdalene: what's in a name?

One of the main clues to Mary's special relationship with Jesus is in her very name: the Magdalene. It is always found with the definite article, *the*, and in Luke 8:2 she's even 'called the Magdalene'. While people could be referred to by means of their provenance (for example, Joseph *of/from* Arimathea in Mark 15:43), in Luke–Acts no one is 'called' a name that indicates provenance.

While it is quite common for people to believe that Mary came from a place named 'Magdala', meaning 'the Tower', there were numerous places called the 'Tower of Something', so we don't have a clear indication of which one it was. They were dotted all around Galilee and wider Judaea. None of them was very important, and so 'Magdala' does not give us a clear place name. Nevertheless, from the fifth century through to Crusader times, Christian pilgrims sought a site called 'Magdala' to venerate Mary, and picked a spot on the shores of the lake in the ruins of an ancient city, perhaps Tarichaea. The Crusaders left that name behind when they left, and it continued to our modern era in a Palestinian fishing village, hence the site of 'Magdala' or 'Migdal' today. But there is no indication that the city of Tarichaea was ever called Magdala in antiquity, and quite good reasons to think it was not.

This is because Mary's name 'Magdalene' wasn't entirely clear to our early Christian scholars, like Origen, Eusebius or Jerome, and they just didn't know about a city supposedly called Magdala. Some wondered if Mary got her name from some obscure village called 'Magdal' (Tower), and some thought it could even indicate Bethany, as a kind of fortified site, because early on Mary

Magdalene was identified with the sister of Martha in Bethany (as found in John 11:1–12:11; Luke 10:38–42). While she is said to have travelled with Jesus from Galilee to Jerusalem, along with many other women, this was not understood to indicate that her home town was in Galilee.

Tellingly, the Christian scholar Jerome, in the fourth century, a man who lived in Bethlehem and knew Hebrew and Aramaic well, said that Mary was not named 'the Magdalene' after a place, but that she was so-named because of her outstanding faith. The word *Magdalaitha*, in Aramaic, is actually based on a root, *gadal*, meaning 'to be great, tall or large' as well as 'raise to dignity', and that may also be packed into the meaning of her epithet. It translates as 'the tower-ess' or 'she who was made great' or 'the aggrandised/magnified one'.

But the ancient people of the Mediterranean loved double-entendres in art and literature, and it is quite possible that Mary was from a village called Magdal-Something (Magdala for short), and yet also gained her particular name 'the Magdalene' not so much because of her provenance but as a special honour, for her towering greatness among the female disciples of Jesus and/or for something about her.

There was a place lying just north of Tiberias named Magdal Nuniyya, 'the Tower of Fish', probably a small fishing village one Sabbath day's journey (about 1.1km) from the northern city gate of Tiberias. This is attested in later rabbinic literature, but may well have existed at the time of Jesus. Standing by the Sea of Galilee today, we can look towards Mount Arbel and think about life in this fishing village and wonder about Mary engaging in this fishing work, like other women disciples of Jesus.

Since Magdalene also indicates greatness or largeness in some way, it is worth noting that in two cases where her name is mentioned it's followed by reference to a healing/exorcism of seven demons (Luke 8:2 and Mark 16:9). Luke has: 'Mary called "Magdalene" from whom seven demons had gone out' as if being called this was thought to have had something to do with the healing or her affliction. Seven demons were a lot to expel, and thus the greatness of her affliction and her successful healing may have been understood by some Aramaic-speakers to account for her special name. There is one parallel to this in a man called Simon the Leper, who hosts Jesus at dinner (Mark 14:3); in playing host, Simon must actually have been healed of his skin disease. The Gerasene man full of many demons gets called 'Legion'. But why does 'the Magdalene' get mentioned in Greek texts without any explanation about such a meaning, rather than 'Mary whose name means "magnified"'? Perhaps this was too dangerous.

As with Salome or Susanna, Mary is never referred to in relation to a man. She was not the wife or mother of someone. She was just Mary (the) Magdalene, alone, and in Luke 8:1–3 she had her own resources. Like other women, here she is shown as having been very ill. She was healed by Jesus, and then she gave up everything to put all her resources into Jesus' mission.

It's hard to imagine what kind of public reaction Mary and the other women would have got for doing all this, at a time when social convention dictated that a woman should be dutiful towards her family and stay at home. It was hardly the mark of a 'good woman' to go off after some charismatic exorcist proclaiming a new age. The fact that Mary would do this, and commit everything to Jesus, shows her utter devotion to him.

Followers and disciples

Some scholars and readers make much of the distinction between a 'follower' of Jesus and a 'disciple', and say that only men were really disciples of Jesus, while women were simply 'followers'. They were pious and devoted but otherwise did nothing of importance. The distinction is important for people who want to argue that only men were properly instructed by Jesus in his teaching and could then teach others, but it is not coherent.

This argument runs counter to what we find in Acts 9:36, where Tabitha is specifically called a 'disciple', and in the Gospel of Peter, where Mary Magdalene is called such. It also runs counter to the fact that in Luke–Acts, people belonging to the Way (i.e., Jesus' disciples) are defined as men and women (Acts 8:1–3; 9:1–4).

> To make a distinction between 'followers' and 'disciples' is not correct. Crowds might literally have followed Jesus in Galilee to seek healing, but his actual 'followers' were his disciples. It was also standard in the ancient world that a disciple would be expected to 'serve' their teacher in return. So finding the terms 'follow' (see Mark 1:16–20) and 'serve' or 'minister to' (see Mark 9:35) linked together are strong indications that the women are Jesus' disciples in Mark 15:41.

In our literature, it's the memory of the special relationship between Mary Magdalene and Jesus that repeats time and time again, even when some of our authors try to shift it and minimise Mary. So the contemporary idea that there is something of a 'love interest' between Jesus and Mary isn't completely off the mark. It's as if people today sense there is a bigger story.

If we go back to the situation of the women on the road with Jesus and the twelve men, ministering, resourcing, engaging with the work of the mission alongside the men, then what was Mary's place? If the named men were sent out 'two by two' in Galilee with female partners, as 'sister wives' in their work, as envoys of Jesus, then did Jesus himself have a female partner to help in his mission, helping to anoint, heal and baptise women? We have to remember again that it was Mary Magdalene who went to the tomb of Jesus in order to do the duties of the closest female relative to the deceased. This was not the job of Jesus' mother or sister; this was her role. Among Jesus' new family of disciples, she was the closest of all women to Jesus. She was the foremost female disciple, and undoubtedly the leader of the women, speaking to other women about Jesus, telling stories, repeating his message, calling them to a new community in anticipation of the coming of the kingdom.

What happened to Mary, then? If Celsus is to be believed, she did have her own following, and this developed in time to the later traditions we have in the *Gospel of Mary*, which is strongly visionary. As a mystic Mary, a teacher Mary, she inspired many. If it were not for her, perhaps we would not even have the Christian faith at all.

5

The Woman with the Flow of Blood
and Other Healed Daughters

The healing of the woman with the flow of blood is one of the most striking narratives in the Christian tradition. It's among the most popular portrayals in early Christian art (see below), occurring thirty-eight times in our surviving images and artefacts (including catacomb paintings, sarcophagi reliefs, amulets, ivories and gems). Taking matters into her own hands, the unnamed woman furtively sneaked up on Jesus from behind, convinced that simply touching his clothes would be enough to heal her. And so it was, though what she didn't expect was that Jesus would feel his

The blood-flow woman with Jesus (early fourth century)

'power' draining from him and demand that she reveal herself. In artistic representations, she's often shown kneeling or bending down as Jesus turns, in a kind of action shot of the dramatic moment: 'Who touched me?'

There is something about this healing that really appealed to people. Perhaps it's because there is more insight into the experience of the person healed than anywhere else – we hear her innermost thoughts and longings and appreciate her as a real person. We feel her frustration with doctors. We feel her relief.

In all three Synoptic Gospels (Mark 5:21–43; Matt. 9:18–25; Luke 8:40–56), the woman's story is framed by another healing – the raising of Jairus' daughter. The two stories have certain themes in common: both are linked by the number twelve (twelve years of suffering for the older woman, twelve years of age for the younger), and both revolve around 'daughters' and feature themes of hopelessness, impurity, touch, healing and salvation (the Greek verb *sozo* means both to heal and to save). The two stories are inextricably interlinked: it's because Jesus stopped to talk to the woman with the flow of blood that he arrived too late to save Jairus' daughter. And their interweaving encourages us to read the two stories together and to reflect on their themes. The story of Jairus' daughter has verbal similarities with the raising of Lazarus and Jesus' own resurrection. Small wonder, then, that artistic representations of the woman with the flow of blood are often linked with images of Lazarus and motifs of resurrection.

Our earliest images of the woman don't tend to give any explicit indication of her affliction. At most, she's situated next to representations of stories of wells or water, obliquely indicating her 'flow' of blood. Very early on, however, it was assumed that she suffered from vaginal or menstrual bleeding, and so was considered impure according to Jewish Law. This made her the perfect example for early church writers to discuss in the context of debates over whether menstruating women could go to church and take the Eucharist. In the third-century *Didascalia Apostolorum* from Syria, the author assures women newly converted from Judaism that there is no need to withdraw from the community while menstruating; Jesus' acceptance of the woman with the flow of blood shows that menstruating women should be admitted.

At the same time, however, Dionysius of Alexandria (a student of Origen's) used the woman to make exactly the opposite argument. He pointed out that the woman only touched the hem of Jesus' garment, and reasoned from this that menstruating women should be kept at a distance. An interesting example of how the same text can be used to support diametrically opposed interpretations!

Even though she is unnamed in the Gospels, in early Christian memory the woman does have a name: Berenice or, in Latin, Veronica. Many people know the much later medieval legend of Veronica, a woman of Jerusalem who gave Jesus a cloth as he laboured under the weight of the cross, stumbling to Golgotha. However, in the earliest stories of Veronica's cloth, as recorded in such works as the *Cure of the Health of Tiberius* (from about the seventh century), the location was Galilee. After she was healed, Veronica had a painter create an image of Jesus, by implication on canvas cloth. Earlier than this, her main role was to testify. In the *Acts of Pilate* and the *Gospel of Nicodemus* (*c.* fifth century), Berenice's task was to witness the amazingness of her own healing.

The name Berenice was clearly attached to the woman by the fourth century, because it was thought that an ancient statue or relief people saw in Paneas (Caesarea Philippi), in northern Palestine, represented Jesus and the blood-flow woman. There seems to have been an inscription giving thanks, providing the name of the woman as Berenice, and an image of a figure identified as Jesus, who was thanked in some way for the healing. It is mentioned in several places, importantly by the fourth-century Christian historian Eusebius of Caesarea (*Ecclesiastical History* 7:18:1–3).

However, this is very unlikely to be a sound memory of the woman's actual name, but rather a case of mistaken identity. Palestine had been a place of huge social upheaval, with cuts in continuities of memory, as places passed from Jewish to pagan to Christian hands.

We know there was indeed a Berenice in the first century, who lived in Caesarea Philippi and is known to have suffered from a malady from which she was cured, but she was a famous queen who lived some decades after Jesus. Queen Berenice was the sister of the Herodian King Agrippa II, and even appears in the New Testament in Acts 25:13, interviewing Paul in Caesarea. The city of Caesarea Philippi was her main base and the location of her palace. As for her malady, the Jewish historian Josephus describes how in the year 66 CE Berenice went to Jerusalem to fulfil a Nazirite vow, since 'it is customary for those suffering from illness or other afflictions to make [such] a vow' (*War* 2:313).

Like other Herodian royalty, Berenice was someone who could move between the worlds of Jerusalem and Rome quite easily, and she and King Agrippa did not subscribe to the usual Jewish practice of banning representational art; Agrippa had his own image placed on coins, and likely also hers, so a representation of Berenice was not surprising. What exactly was shown on the statue or relief in Paneas may be hard to pin down, but since Jesus in the fourth century was commonly represented as a kind of Asclepius, the god of healing shown with long hair, a beard and a long robe, it was perhaps natural for Christians to view a statue of the healing god as the image of the healing Son of God. The long-haired, long-robed Jesus became increasingly recognised as an image of Jesus in the fourth century.

Sex and gender

Normatively, in ancient Judaism, the observed physical female body mapped on to being classified as a 'woman' or 'girl'. The duality of male and female was strongly connected with the capacity for reproduction. Observed bodily characteristics at birth led to subsequent gendered categorisations and expected behaviours. Being classified as a male (and not a female) was dependent on having observable male sex organs, importantly a penis that could be circumcised on the eighth day.

As today, there were people who were intersex, who were understood as being both male and female (with legal obligations of both sexes), and those who were neither male nor female. The Jewish rabbis acknowledged at least some intersex people as being in a category of their own, if they had anatomy of both

---

sexes, but in terms of gender they were to dress like men (Mishnah Bikkurim 4; Tosefta Bikkurim 2:3–7), which would lead to their commonly perceived gender identity.

Someone classified as male at birth who did not develop a beard and body hair by the age of eighteen or twenty could be deemed a 'eunuch', a saris (Mishnah, Niddah 5:9; Yevamot 8:4), rather than reclassified as female. Someone classified as female at birth who did develop hair could be called an ailonit, a 'female ram' (Babylonian Talmud, Ketubbot 11a), who is also 'barren'. But identity as male or female, once given, remained fixed, unless that identity was as someone androgynous at birth, who nevertheless was required to present as a man in appearance.

It seems that Jesus could play around with gender categories. He noted that there were 'eunuchs' who were born this way (i.e., inter-sex people) and even advised his male disciples to be like them for the sake of the kingdom, in not marrying (Matt. 19:12). In a much-debated saying in the Gospel of Thomas *(114), Peter announced, 'Let Mary go out from us, for females are not worthy of the life', and Jesus responded by saying he 'will make her male so that she might become a living spirit like you males, for every female who makes herself male will enter the Kingdom of Heaven.'*

In this patriarchal world, we need to remember that angels were understood as males, so Mary was proclaimed as destined to be like an angel in the kingdom. In fact, in Matthew 22:30, Jesus stated, 'In the resurrection they [masc.] do not marry nor are they [fem.] given in marriage, but they are like the angels in heaven.' In Luke 20:34–35 the saying appears as: 'The children of this world marry [masc.] and are given in marriage [fem.], but those who are judged worthy of a space in the other world and in the resurrection of the dead do not marry [masc.], because they can no longer die. For they are the same as angels and, being children of the resurrection, they are sons of God.' In this case, the categories of male and female apply only in the present world, not in the kingdom.

Healing women of infirmities and evil spirits

We've already looked at the key passage in Luke 8:2 where we're told that there were many women who followed, served and resourced Jesus and his mission. Unlike in Mark, Luke adds that these women 'had been cured of evil spirits and infirmities'. With these words, a reason is given for the extraordinary actions of these women, as if to justify why they would do something so radical as to be on the road with Jesus, giving away their possessions and money to the movement. Jesus had healed them of conditions that seemed impossible to cure, and so they were prepared to do anything for him.

While their names are unknown, we do have a few healing stories in the Gospels that focus on other women. We've already met Peter's unnamed mother-in-law and seen how, after she was healed, she 'served' or 'ministered' to Jesus and his companions (Mark 1:29–31, also found in Matt. 8:14–15; Luke 4:38–39). In the context, it looks as if she provided hospitality by serving dinner to a group of men: Jesus, Peter, Andrew, James and John.

But what if this story should be read as reflecting a broader response, as we have in Luke 8, that she provided *ongoing* service to them in the new mission? The story is located soon after the male disciples were called to become 'fishers of people', at a time when Jesus was gathering disciples. The healing itself must have been extraordinary. In the Gospel of Mark, Jesus 'came and grasped her hand and raised her up', in a way that indicates close physical touch. What if this healing functioned as a kind of call to her own discipleship?

In Luke there's a story of another unnamed woman who was beset by 'a spirit of infirmity' that had crippled her for eighteen years, so that she was bent over double and unable to stand up straight. She was in a synagogue where Jesus was teaching on the Sabbath. He called to her, 'Woman, you are released from your infirmity.' Immediately she was able to stand up straight, and she praised God. While the ruler of the synagogue was bothered that Jesus had 'worked' by healing on the Sabbath, the day of rest, Jesus replied, 'Shouldn't this daughter of Abraham, that Satan has bound for eighteen years, be freed from this binding on the Sabbath?' (Luke 13:10–17). In calling her a 'daughter of Abraham', Jesus validated her faith, since Abraham was the prime model of trust in God. The term 'daughter' shows Jesus' love and compassion for the woman, and underscores the familial relationship among those who were gathering around him.

The mention of 'a spirit of infirmity' shows that the distinction between 'evil spirits' and 'infirmities' in Luke 8:2 was not hard and fast. In the folk medicine of Galilee at the time of Jesus, people believed that evil spirits – demons – caused illness, and that you could lay yourself open to demonic attack by behaving badly ('sinning'). A good example is in the story of the man born blind in John 9, where discussion surrounded the question of who had sinned in this case, the man (who had never been able to see) or his parents (John 9:2–3).

Repentance from bad behaviour was considered to be a prelude to healing: God had to forgive a person for their sins (see the healing of the paralysed man in Mark 2:1–12 for an explicit articulation of this). Jesus operated according to the beliefs of this time, healing people by casting out such unclean evil spirits by the pure Holy Spirit. He could mediate forgiveness and could wield this Spirit (and transfer the Spirit to others). The healings were both acts of compassion and means by which Jesus proved he was truly sent with divine power, and they underscored his divine message of the imminent kingdom, the soon-to-be-realised new world order that would be as God wanted it to be.

We know of this contemporary folk medicine from other sources outside the Gospels, and we even have pictures of demons drawn on magic bowls, from slightly later times. It was often thought male demons particularly attacked girls and women, and female demons particularly attacked boys and men. There was a whole science surrounding demons and what particular maladies they caused, from headaches and tummy upsets to emotional and mental distress, all listed in an ancient work known as the *Testament of Solomon*. Demons were considered to occupy the body, like burglars taking over a house and binding up the householders. In the case of the 'daughter of Abraham' in Luke 13, Jesus used the language of binding and freeing (loosing). He brought her not only relief, but also liberation.

A good exorcist would be able to identify the demon(s), call them by their name and command them to depart by various means: by calling upon an angel, by driving them out with a potion or other substance, or by incantations. The exorcist could effectively bind up the demons or cast them out into the wilderness. This was not just a Judaean belief; many amulets (worn for protection) and papyri have been found around the Mediterranean with spells and incantations designed for tackling such demons. Demons were around and about everywhere, like germs and viruses today.

Jesus frequently healed through touch in the Gospels, and is sometimes shown using special ointment (for example, the saliva on the tongue of the deaf man in Mark 7:33 and the eyes of the blind man in Mark 8:23), or even 'magical' words (such as the Aramaic in Mark 5:41 or 7:34). In general, though, the Gospel writers tend to tone down Jesus' actions. Presumably the reason for this is to distance Jesus from any possible charge of 'magic' or 'sorcery' – an accusation we know that opponents were only too quick to bring against him. The Gospel of Luke is particularly keen to show that Jesus simply commanded the demons with his authoritative words rather than engaging in anything 'hands on'. So, for example, in the healing of Peter's mother-in-law, the Lukan version (4:39) notes that Jesus 'rebuked the fever' rather than 'grasped her hand' as we have it in Mark (1:31). Similarly, with the crippled woman in the synagogue, it may well be that in the original story adapted by Luke there was a more tactile engagement by Jesus in the woman's cure – perhaps he put his hands on her bent back.

Whatever the case, if we consider the foundation of this story to be accurate, let's think about the woman's experience. This woman, who had been bent over for eighteen years, couldn't have been expecting an easy cure after that long. She would have been unable to work like other women, and no doubt suffered great pain. The experience of being freed from an ailment that had long afflicted her may well have made her want to give Jesus and his mission everything she had, and she would have testified to people about her healing. In this way, healed women like her, on the road with Jesus, could become part of his campaign. They could impart important details like, 'I was bent over double with this terrible back pain for eighteen years! Now look at me!' The detail of the period of time she suffered from her affliction could only have come from the woman herself. In the case of the woman with the flow of blood, too, we're told explicitly how long she had suffered. What's fascinating about this story, however, is the insight we're given into the woman's thoughts and experience.

The woman with the flow of blood

The earliest version of this story is told in Mark, and it's retold in Matthew and in Luke with certain tweaks (Mark 5:24b–34 = Matt. 9:20–22 = Luke 8.42b–48). We read here of a woman who apparently had a never-ending flow of blood, though we do not know whether this was heavy or light. The condition might have been the result of endometriosis, fibroids or polyps, or another type of underlying condition. It is unclear how much blood she was losing, but even a small amount continually coming out of her on a daily basis would not only have been worrying, but it would also have been exhausting.

In addition, she would have been in a state of ritual impurity. According to the Mosaic Law, women bleeding either during their monthly periods or after childbirth were impure, and were not allowed to touch anything consecrated or permitted in the Sanctuary. Furthermore, they were not only impure but transmitted uncleanness to other people (Lev. 12:1–8; 15:19–33; 20:18). A menstruating woman's impurity (*niddah*) was one thing, but a woman who continued to have a blood flow outside her menstrual period was called a *zavah*, as also someone suffering from gonorrhoea. In Numbers 5:1–4, Moses was instructed to expel anyone from the camp with a continual discharge, male or female. In the time of Jesus, that may well have set a standard for the holy city of

Jerusalem and the Temple, or among certain schools (like those responsible for the Temple Scroll, among the Dead Sea Scrolls), but this should probably not lead us to think she was completely socially excluded and living out on her own in Galilee. Menstruating women and women having just given birth were at home; the onus was placed on those who wanted to stay pure to be careful around them and where they sat or lay.

There is a question about how much ordinary people would have attended to such purity regulations beyond what was required for visiting the Temple in Jerusalem. The legal schools like the Pharisees and Essenes appear to have been particularly fastidious about maintaining standards of purity in daily life, but farm workers and fisherfolk not so much. So, certainly the woman's impurity would have excluded her from making pilgrimage visits to the holy city, but perhaps few other restrictions.

In terms of sexual relations, a man aiming to maintain purity was not permitted to have sex with a menstruating woman. This would have meant that the woman in this story could not have sexual relations or conceive. Her condition alone may have made conception impossible. She may well in this case have been divorced as a result, if she had ever been married.

Medically, she would have been run down: any continual blood loss could result in anaemia, especially in an environment in which a good diet could not be guaranteed. There is no mention of any husband or sons or wider family of the woman in this story. The most natural inference is that she was unmarried, either never married (because of her condition) or divorced. But she had, or had had, her own money, though it had been wasted on physicians.

In the story in Mark, a large crowd was pressing in on Jesus as he was walking along. A woman 'who had been suffering from a flow of blood for twelve years' was there. As with the bent-over woman, she must have told people about her suffering for twelve years. There is also this detail: 'She'd suffered a great deal by (the treatment of) many physicians and spent all of her (money), without having got better in any way at all, but rather she'd got worse.' That sounds like exactly what she would say to people, in terms

84

Barrenness and the stigma of divorce

In the ancient world, ordinary women did not generally have a good time with divorce. Elite women could manage if they had their own money, but many women did not have such private funds. They would enter marriage with a dowry that could be used by their husbands, and part of this could be returned in the case of divorce, but that depended on whether there was anything left. Their children usually stayed with their ex-husband's family.

It was shameful to be divorced; a woman was effectively 'fired' from her job. In Judaea, only a man had a legal right to initiate divorce and a woman could be divorced for many reasons, including not falling pregnant. Male infertility was not recognised, while 'barrenness' for a woman was a serious misfortune (see Isa. 54:1). The Jewish philosopher Philo, a contemporary of Jesus, actually commented compassionately on the obligation to divorce a 'barren' woman, and took pity on men who remain married to their barren wives because of the power of familiarity, but he had no sympathy at all for men who married women who had previously been shown to be barren (Special Laws 3:32–34).

As with women whose husbands had died, divorced women could be referred to as cherai, *'widows' (Philo, Special Laws 2:25–31).*

---

of what she had put up with. There is even an indication of her thoughts. She'd heard the news about Jesus and so 'she said (to herself), "If I could only touch his mantle I will be healed."' So she came up behind Jesus and reached out to touch it. Clearly, she knew about Jesus touching people to heal them, with a power of healing that came from this.

What's truly remarkable – and unique – about this story is that her cure seemed to happen without Jesus' knowledge! As soon as her hand touched his mantle, 'immediately her flow of blood dried up' and she knew she was cured. It was only after this – after the woman was cured – that Jesus felt that power had gone out of him, and looking around him asked, 'Who touched my clothes?'

His disciples, apparently close by, quite rudely retort, 'Look at the crowd pressing on you, and you say, "Who touched me?"'

At this point 'the woman, knowing what had been done to her, came in fear and trembling and fell down before him, and told him the whole truth'.

Jesus said, 'Daughter, your faith has saved you; go in peace and be healed of your affliction.' As with the bent-over woman in the synagogue, she too was a 'daughter' of Abraham, because of her faith in Jesus.

How did she feel? There is no explicit mention of purity in the story as we have it (though some of the language of the 'flow' echoes the passage in Leviticus), but that does not mean it was not a factor in her real experience. It makes her initiative to reach out and touch Jesus even bolder. Rather than her impurity contaminating him, his pure, healing Spirit was drawn out to dry up the source of her ailment and her uncleanness. The dirty demon was evicted, the flow was 'dried up' and she was purified in her womb, deep inside her. A channel of energy flowed from Jesus to the woman's inner parts, without him even consciously willing it. Her faith was so great she knew that Jesus was a direct conduit of the divine, full of health-giving, demon-evicting purity.

The woman's testimony to this healing would have been vital. While the bent-over woman could stand up straight for all to see, the woman with the flow of blood *felt* it, at that moment. Presumably later on people would have confirmed that she was not continually laundering her menstrual rags, and had immersed herself in a ritual bath, but the story is all about what happened there and then. What she said on the spot concerning 'the whole truth' was one thing, but such a story would have been repeated and repeated.

These daughters of Abraham, full of faith, proved the power Jesus had to bring the healing promise of the kingdom, and shared their experience as outreach. This is also a remarkable story for the woman taking the initiative, going in individually for a touch of Jesus' garment (likely in fact one of the tassels at the four corners of his mantle, as Mark 6:56 suggests). The woman's voice lies just behind this telling, and we even have her thoughts represented as speech.

It's also interesting to see how the story is retold, to note how the stories of women get changed. Matthew and Luke have shortened versions, and the woman's complaint about physicians is dropped, though in Luke it is noted that 'she couldn't get healed by anyone'. Jesus is presented more favourably, as knowing more about what is going on. In Matthew, Jesus identified her immediately and didn't need to ask who touched him. In Luke, the women gave her testimony right away to everyone around: 'And when the woman saw that she was not hidden, she came trembling, and falling down before him declared in the presence of all the people why she had touched him, and how she had been immediately healed' (Luke 8:47).

Also in Luke there is an interesting parallel between what Jesus said to her and what he said to the 'sinner' who washed his feet with her tears. Here Jesus said, 'Daughter, your faith has saved/cured you. Go in peace.' To the 'sinner' he said, 'Your faith has saved/cured you. Go in peace' (Luke 7:50). This prompts readers to link the two stories, and in fact they do have similarities in that in both cases women took the initiative and touched Jesus without asking, showing more faith in Jesus than anyone else around.

A woman teaches Jesus

If the woman with the flow of blood seized the initiative, another seemed to teach him an important lesson. The story focuses on a non-Jewish woman: Mark calls her a Greek, a Syro-Phoenician (Mark 7:24–30); Matthew calls her a Canaanite (Matt. 15:21–28). Jesus met her in Gentile territory, just after he had been explaining to his disciples that eating with unwashed hands (like the Gentiles) didn't matter anymore' (Mark 7: 1–23).

Jesus was tired and retired to a house to rest, but the woman sought him out and begged him to heal her daughter. The rest of the scene focuses more on the exchange between Jesus and the unnamed woman than the exorcism itself, which is narrated almost as an afterthought at the end. At first, Jesus refused the woman's request, rudely referring to her and her daughter as 'dogs'.

Attempts to lessen the insult here – to translate the word as 'puppies' or to suggest that Jesus had a teasing smile on his face – don't work. Despite his earlier teaching, Jesus couldn't initially see that this Gentile woman's faith had earned her and her daughter a place in the kingdom. It seems to have been common for Jews to refer to Gentiles as 'dogs' (and doubtless they gave back as good as they got). The woman had probably received this kind of put-down all her life, but she refused to let Jesus have the last word. Referring to him with respect (*Kurie*: 'Lord' or 'Sir'), she acknowledged that the children (Jews) had the privileged place, but argued that this didn't stop the dogs under the table (non-Jews, like her and her child) sharing the leftovers. Jesus had to accept that her argument got the better of him and he healed her daughter. It was clearly her words here, rather than her faith, that did the trick.

Although Jesus seemed to know in theory that the message could be taken to Gentiles, it took this woman to turn his words to actions. The image of the leftovers anticipates the feedings of the five thousand and the four thousand – where Jews and Gentiles shared equally in the banquet (the feeding of the five thousand took place on Jewish soil while the feeding of the four thousand seems to have occurred in Gentile territory, suggesting that the evangelists have both groups in mind). While it may be too much to suggest that the woman's refusal to accept Jesus' churlish rejection changed the course of his ministry, her clever answer may have helped him to see the logical consequences of his own teaching. She was rewarded when she returned home to find her daughter freed from her demon and lying on her bed.

So we return to the women on the road with Jesus, healed of various infirmities, cleansed of dirty demons, free from their afflictions, and eager to tell people about what had happened. They were an important part of Jesus' team of witnesses, proclaiming the meaning of the kingdom. As Jesus sent his envoys out to ask people to repent, cast out demons, anoint the sick with oil and heal them (Mark 6:13), what a difference the testimony of the women would have made in the way people responded.

6

Martha and Mary

Taking their cue from the short story in Luke, most people today think of Mary and Martha as the embodiment of two different responses to Jesus. Mary represents the contemplative, thoughtful way, exemplified by the spiritual life, holy orders and the convent. Martha embodies an active, practical response epitomised by the 'lady helpers' at church gatherings and social committees. But the two ways are not equal: Jesus' declaration that Mary has chosen 'the better part' serves to undermine typical 'woman's work', rendering it secondary and inconsequential. It's no surprise that the female servants of the dystopian society created by Margaret Atwood in *The Handmaid's Tale* are called 'Marthas'.

Martha's active lifestyle hasn't always been held against her. In the thirteenth century, the *Golden Legend* told how she made her way to Marseilles in a rudderless boat, along with her brother Lazarus and sister Mary (who was identified with Mary Magdalene). The siblings, all now boasting noble ancestry, settled in Provence and set about converting the locals to the faith. In other traditions Martha became a Gallic saint with great powers of healing, and is even credited with taming a dragon that was terrorising the countryside. She's remembered as an independent virgin, intelligent, strong and socially defiant. Her actions were more typical of male saints, such as the ubiquitous St George, who similarly armed himself against the dragon with a cross and a prayer. As with Mary Magdalene, Martha could be reinvented in various ways. In the late fourth century, Bishop Ambrose of Milan went against the prevailing trend of identifying the blood-flow woman as Berenice, and linked her instead with Martha (*On Solomon* 46:14; *Oration* 5:42–43).

But what were the sisters really like? A close look at the ancient texts suggests two active female disciples at the very heart of the new movement.

Competing sisters

Turning to the biblical accounts, in the Gospel of Luke there is a single story involving Martha and Mary, set amid Jesus' Galilean ministry (Luke 10:38–42). As Jesus was on his way, Martha welcomed him into her home. Her sister Mary sat at Jesus' feet and listened to what he had to say. But Martha was 'distracted with much serving' and appealed to Jesus to tell her sister to lend a hand. Jesus refused to take Martha's side, remarking only, 'Martha, Martha, you are worried and distracted by many things; there is need of only one thing. Mary has chosen the better part, which will not be taken away from her.'

Martha

The name Martha is found in texts and on ossuaries (bone boxes) from around the time of Jesus. It actually means 'Mistress', or 'Lady', in Aramaic. This makes it look like the equivalent to Mar, *'Master' or 'Lord', which was a way of addressing Jesus. His Aramaic-speaking disciples prayed for his presence by saying* 'Marana tha', *'Our Lord, come' (1 Cor. 16:22). However, Martha does seem to be just a name, not necessarily a title. Calling a girl 'Lady' indicated perhaps a special value given to a daughter, maybe the eldest of a family.*

The anecdote ends here, with Jesus' grandiose pronouncement, and we are left to wonder about Martha's response. Did she feel put down and humiliated? Accused of 'fussing' (never a good thing in a woman) and missing the point of Jesus' visit? Yet how could she invite this man into her home without showing him hospitality? And all the while, of course, sister Mary sat smugly, failing to help and being commended for it. Even sisters, it seems, couldn't pull together.

It might come as a surprise to those familiar with this story to realise that food and cooking aren't actually mentioned. In the Greek, Martha is distracted with much 'serving'. The important word, which we have met before, is *diakoneo*, related to the word 'deacon' (*diakonos*). While it can mean 'waiting at tables', it can also mean rendering service and support in all kinds of ways, and when used of a man it's more commonly translated as 'ministry'. In due course, being a *diakonos* was thought of as a 'sacred commission'. (The 'deacons' in Acts 6 are a good example of this double meaning: although appointed to wait on tables in order to settle a dispute, they actually occupied themselves with preaching and teaching.) Martha engaging in '*much* serving' implies she was not just catering to Jesus, but also to a whole group who had come with him into her home. We remember Jesus was accompanied by a throng of disciples, men and women (and children).

Elsewhere in Luke, *diakoneo* refers to the public roles of mission and proclamation, as well as practical serving, so why not here? This would put Luke's story in an entirely different light. Rather than a dispute about household chores, the quarrel is now about Christian ministry, in all its forms. Mary was sitting among Jesus' crowd, on the floor 'at Jesus' feet' (since he was on a chair), listening to him. In validating Mary's decision, Jesus was saying, 'Listen first, serve later', not, 'Listen only, don't serve'. After all, he himself was one who served.

The language of service is crucial in our texts. We might suspect that this story was included because it was saying something to the church of Luke's own day in the late first century. But what exactly?

If this were a dispute between two men, we'd likely conclude that the story was making a point about ministry in general. The moral might then be something along the lines of, don't allow the practical details of running a congregation to hinder the important thing – hearing the word of Jesus.

But we remember that women were not a good feature for people like Celsus. Does this passage also try to hide the women disciples by not telling us the whole story? It is true that Mary was commended for listening to Jesus, and she was allowed to learn, but we never see Mary passing on her knowledge to anyone else. And Martha quite clearly had her 'ministry' curtailed; she was told she was too worried, as if it was too much for her, that she was overburdened, and that the proper way for women to conduct themselves was through listening. This reading chimes very closely with the account of Christian congregations in Acts: although women are well represented, they are rarely presented as preachers, missionaries or founders of house churches.

We've already seen that women were prominent in the Jesus movement from the start (an impression that will be confirmed by Paul's letters that refer to women in leadership positions, as we'll see in Chapter 11). *Might the author or redactor of the present passage have wanted to curtail women's activities within the Church?* We have to remember that stories could be told and retold in different contexts, and manuscripts could be edited and re-edited.

In the compilation of our New Testament books, there are passages that clearly try to limit women's roles. For example, in 1 Timothy 2:12, the author maintains, 'I permit no woman to teach or to have authority over a man; she is to keep silent.' Why say this, unless women *were* teaching and assuming authority within the congregation over men as well as women? Luke–Acts would then include a story in which Jesus was made to limit women's ministry, namely Martha's. And this is done by drawing on some of the oldest female stereotypes in existence: the competing sisters who need to appeal to a male authority figure to judge between them. What this story shows, of course, is that women were still active in church ministry at this period.

In feminist reading, all this is called a 'hermeneutic of suspicion' ('hermeneutic' here just means 'interpretation'; see the box on this topic in Chapter 5 above). We are suspicious of presentations of women in texts reflecting patriarchal worldviews, and ask whether the text is written to commend a particular type of (female) behaviour, rather than simply reporting events as they happened. However, if we think about this story as preserving in some part an authentic memory of two women who were disciples of Jesus, maybe we can also salvage an important vindication of their activity. They were so important and influential that this story had to be told to limit them.

Even with the limitations, there is no question that they were disciples, and they behaved in an autonomous way. Martha was on such familiar terms with Jesus that she reprimanded him and told him what to do! 'Master, don't you care that my sister has left me to serve alone? Tell her to help me.' Mary decided to sit as a disciple at Jesus' feet, a role often seen as only for men and boys. If we read 'serving' in traditional terms, Mary was affirmed at that moment as having the right not to do traditional women's work of serving in another part of the house, where she could not hear him.

Jesus himself in Luke is a 'server' (Luke 22:27): 'Who is more important – the one who sits at table or the one serving? Isn't it the one sitting at table? But I am among you as one serving.' It really doesn't fit with this statement that he should have had no sympathy with Martha, and done nothing to help her as one who served. So should we really understand that Martha was actually given permission to leave off this traditional serving for a while, and listen with her sister? Perhaps after the teaching was done they would all serve together?

Diego Rodriguez di Silva y Velasquez, Christ in the House of Martha and Mary *(1618)*

This actually tells us something very important. There are different ways of interpreting a story. The reason for the inclusion of a story in a Gospel and certain tweaking can be one thing, but the story itself at core can point us to a different reading. Mary and Martha's rights to sit with other (male and female) disciples and learn would prepare them ultimately to be adept in Jesus' teaching. It was expected that disciples would study and memorise their teacher's words, so that they could accurately impart them to others. An indication that we are on the right lines here comes from our second biblical passage, where Martha and Mary are held up as prominent examples of early church leaders.

Martha's recognition of Jesus

Martha and Mary appear again in the Gospel of John, in a much lengthier treatment. Of all his female characters, John devotes most time to Martha and Mary, attributing great insight to each of them.

The sisters appear first in connection with the raising of their brother Lazarus in Bethany (John 11:1–46). Curiously, John needs to explain who Lazarus was, but seems to assume that his audience would know of 'Mary and her sister Martha'. The sisters sent a message to Jesus, alerting him to the painful fact that their brother was ill. Despite his love for all three of them, however, Jesus waited a couple of days until he visited, arriving only after Lazarus had been in the tomb for four days.

The characterisation of Martha as the more dynamic sister persists into this Gospel, where she went out to meet Jesus on the road, accosting him with the charge that if he had been there her brother would not have died. 'Your brother will rise again,' Jesus said, which Martha took to refer to the general resurrection that most Jews expected on the 'last day'. But this was not at all what Jesus meant. 'I am the resurrection and the life,' he declared. 'Those who believe in me, even though they die, will live, and everyone who lives and believes in me will never die. Do you believe this?'

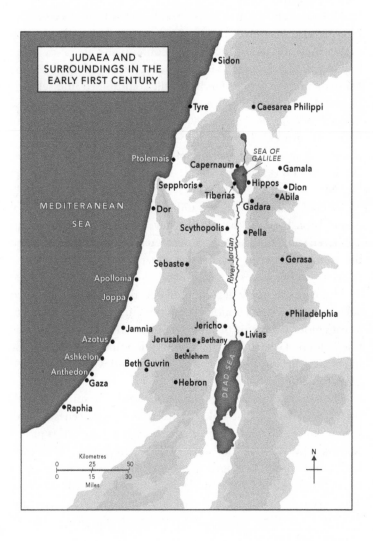

Martha's response is a high point of the Gospel so far: 'Yes, Lord, I believe that you are the Messiah, the Son of God, the one coming into the world.'

All too often Martha's confession here has been dismissed by interpreters. Scenes featuring women are frequently seen as 'light relief', devoid of theological content, and are rarely given much weight. Despite Martha's recognition of Jesus as the Messiah and the Son of God, it's still common to find scholars pointing out that she had no idea that Jesus was about to raise her brother. A comparison with Matthew's Gospel is useful here. At around halfway through the narrative (as here), Matthew's Jesus asked the disciples who they thought he was. Peter's confession was startlingly similar to Martha's: 'You are the Messiah, the Son of the living God.' He was not only commended for his understanding but also given a special commission by Jesus to hold the keys of heaven (Matt. 16:13–20). Even some of the earliest interpreters of John's Gospel noted the parallels between Martha and Peter here, with at least one referring to her as a 'second Peter'.

This is a remarkable depiction of an early female disciple, even acknowledging John's uniformly positive attitude towards women. What's more, the raising of Lazarus takes on an important symbolic role in John's Gospel. In a concrete way, it points towards the raising of all believers, all those 'loved' by the Lord who will be raised to eternal life.

The raising of Lazarus also points forward to Jesus' own death (there are close verbal links between the two scenes). Small wonder, then, that many early Christian writers and artists placed Martha and Mary at the tomb of Jesus. In Eastern Orthodox tradition the sisters belonged to the 'myrrh-bearers', the group of women who buried Jesus and later discovered the empty tomb. Their contribution is remembered and commemorated throughout the Holy Week celebrations, but specifically on the second Sunday after Easter.

A second-century work known as the *Epistula Apostolorum*, purporting to be a letter from the eleven remaining disciples, describes the visit of the sisters to Jesus' tomb and their commissioning by the risen Jesus to take the good news to the disciples (a scene reminiscent of the one involving Mary Magdalene in John 20). In one mystical poem from the early third century, written by Hippolytus of Rome, Martha was with Mary (Magdalene) at the tomb. In this work, known as the *Commentary on the Song of Songs*, the two women together spoke Mary Magdalene's words in John 20:16, 'Rabbouni', and attempted to grasp hold of Christ's feet to prevent him from ascending. When the male disciples did not believe Martha and Mary, Jesus appeared and stated, 'It was my desire, I who appeared to these women, to send them also as apostles to you.' Martha, then, as one of the female 'apostles to the apostles', has a high place in early Christian memory, along with Mary Magdalene.

Moreover, an amulet from sixth- or seventh-century Egypt depicts a crucifixion scene with Martha and Mary holding incense in the lower part of the design. Along with the women's names, the text reads, 'Cross, protect Aba Moun'. The amulet, now in the Cabinet des Médailles in France, was clearly worn for protection, to keep the bearer safe from harm, but the presence of the two sisters is an intriguing clue to the significance that they must have retained among at least some believers even many centuries later.

Mary's anointing of Jesus

The connection between the sisters and anointing takes us back to John's account of the other sister, Mary. In the Lazarus story she played second fiddle to her more talkative sister. True to type, as set in Luke, she remained in the house at first, only interacting with Jesus when she was brought to him by Martha. The depth of her grief and emotion had a profound effect on Jesus, who also began to cry. Perhaps the story reassured John's readers that grief was still an appropriate response to the death of a loved one, even among faithful disciples who knew that those loved ones would be raised to eternal life.

Mary's principal scene is her anointing of Jesus (John 12), though curiously she is introduced a whole chapter earlier with the intriguing statement that 'it was Mary who anointed the Lord with ointment and wiped his feet with her hair' (John 11:2). It seems to be one of the statements in the Gospel that points outside the narrative, so that readers are supposed to go, 'Aha!'

As it stands, this looks to be the story of the anointing 'sinner' in Luke 7:36–50. We will think more about the relationships between the different anointing stories in the next chapter. In John, Mary repeated her action, and this time the anointing occurred six days before the last, fateful Passover, when Jesus came once more to the sisters' home in Bethany. Lazarus played host while Martha characteristically (from Luke) served. During the meal, Mary brought in a large amount of costly perfume and anointed Jesus' feet, wiping them with her hair. She used so much perfume that the whole house was filled with the fragrance. Judas Iscariot, who would betray Jesus, piped up and asked why she had wasted so much money that could have been given to the poor. (It's explained that this wasn't because he cared about the poor but because he kept the common purse and stole from it.)

Jesus defended Mary. Perhaps we are to think she saw her extravagant gift as a sign of love, a mark of her complete devotion to the Teacher who had turned her life upside down.

There are also strong hints here of self-denial and humiliation. Washing or anointing feet was considered demeaning for all but the lowest slaves or female family members. By anointing Jesus' *feet*, then, Mary demonstrated her utterly selfless commitment to Jesus. Shortly after this story, Jesus spent his last evening with his disciples where he – significantly – washed their feet. Mary's actions had anticipated those of Jesus; are we to understand that he had learnt to behave in this way from her (as he learnt earlier from the Syro-Phoenician woman, see Chapter 5)?

Let's remember, too, that our early Christian literature equates Mary the sister of Martha with Mary Magdalene. In fact, the Gospel of John strongly leads us in the direction of this equation. Given that after Mary anointed Jesus' feet with pure nard and was challenged by Judas, Jesus replied, 'Leave her alone; let her keep it for the day of my burial' (John 12:7), we would expect her to be present on the day of Jesus' burial. Instead, we have the women at the cross and the 'disciple Jesus loved'.

At the burial, later that day, no women were involved, just Joseph of Arimathea and Nicodemus, who brought a huge amount (100 litras/pounds) of myrrh and aloes and bound up Jesus' body with these (John 19:38–42). But then Mary 'the Magdalene' came to the tomb on the first day of the week while it was still dark (20:1). She just turned up. No perfume is mentioned, but it seems as if Mary had duly kept perfume for the day of burial, and then came to the tomb anyway. Other than that, no further motive is given for Mary coming to the tomb. It is only in Mark that it is explained that the women came to the tomb 'so that they might go and anoint him' (Mark 16:1), but in John that job has been done by Nicodemus. Given what Jesus says regarding saving the nard, if Mary was *not* at the tomb following through with this, then the narrative would have an unexplained substitution of Marys.

Mary the sister of Martha is slightly marginalised, upstaged by her sister in John 11, yet it is stated that Jesus did have a special relationship with the siblings. They were all disciples whom Jesus loved. We're told that Jesus loved 'Martha, and her sister, and Lazarus' (John 11:5, see also verse 36) and all were disciples in having Jesus as their 'Teacher' (John 11:28). So no wonder Mary Magdalene then called the risen Jesus 'Teacher'.

Some scholars argue that it would actually follow quite well in the narrative that Lazarus was the 'disciple Jesus loved', since he is the only man to be defined as being loved by Jesus specifically. The sisters even sent a message to Jesus that 'he whom you love is ill' (John 11:3).

However, just because the author of the Gospel of John alluded to Mary Magdalene being Mary the sister of Martha (and even the sinner of Luke 7), that does not necessarily mean we should follow suit. We remember that 'Mary' was an extremely common name. We need to go back to the story of the anointing woman as first told in the Gospel of Mark to retrieve more of the reality, as we shall see in the next chapter.

Real women

What, then, can we piece together of the historical women behind these texts and memories? Much, of course, has to be guesswork, but a number of significant features are clear enough. It's surely noteworthy that two evangelists remember these women, with John devoting a great deal of space to their relationship with Jesus. It seems reasonable to conclude that the sisters were prominent disciples, whose role in the early Jesus movement could not be brushed aside.

It's also interesting that neither of them was connected with a man (except, of course, Lazarus). At a time when women were defined by their male relationships, moving through life in stages as first the daughter of, then wife of, and finally the mother of men, it is noteworthy that neither sister appears to have been married. Their decision to follow Jesus was clearly their own, not that of a more dominant male.

The women's link to Bethany seems strong. Although Luke sets his story in the midst of the Galilee material, he doesn't actually give it any particular setting (and we might suspect that the relocation is part of an attempt to reduce the importance of the sisters). John is clear that their home was in Bethany, and this is reinforced by the presence of a 'guest house' there that became a place of pilgrimage. The remains of this 'guest house' are now located in the grounds of the Sisters of Mercy convent in Bethany, where a Byzantine cave covered in graffiti testifies to the high reverence in which it was held for a long time.

The intrepid nun Egeria, who travelled around the Holy Land in the third century, talks of services being held at the place where Martha and Mary met Jesus (*Travels* 29:3–6). It is possible, of course, that the cave's veneration is simply inspired by John's story, and is nothing more than an understandable desire on the part of pilgrims to associate sacred texts with concrete places. Yet we should not automatically jump to this conclusion; places and traditions can live on for long periods of time in popular memory and folklore, and there may well be an ancient connection between the sisters and this particular site. Undoubtedly, pilgrims came to see the place where Jesus had raised Lazarus from the dead, but it is tempting to imagine that some visitors derived support and encouragement from the memory of the two sisters who had once lived there, perhaps drawing inspiration from both their grief and their faith. The presence of graffiti in the cave, some of it directly imploring the two sisters, strongly suggests that this was, in fact, the case.

Bethany was a village close to Jerusalem, on the eastern side of the Mount of Olives, and would have been a handy place to stay for anyone visiting the holy city. At Passover, thousands of Jews came to Jerusalem from all over the eastern Mediterranean. As Jerusalem was a walled city, there was a limit to how many could squeeze into its guest rooms and hostelries; some camped outside the walls, under canvas, while others preferred to stay in surrounding villages such as Bethany and Bethphage.

The suggestion (corroborated by Mark) that Jesus and his probably large group of disciples stayed out in Bethany is quite plausible. There would have been more space there for them to stay comfortably, and more protection in what was quickly becoming a highly charged atmosphere. The walk into the city was only two miles, and plenty of others would have joined them on the road. Luke is quite clear that the house was Martha's, suggesting a strong tradition that she was the owner of a house in the environs of Jerusalem where Jesus and his supporters were remembered to have stayed. And if John's Gospel is correct to suggest that Jesus actually went to the holy city quite often, then he would presumably have been a regular guest at the house.

One intriguing question surrounds their 'sisterhood'. Were they biological sisters, sisters-in-law or sisters in the faith? Paul, of course, talks of fellow believers as 'brothers and sisters' or 'siblings'. If the latter, they may have been a missionary pair such as Tryphaena and Tryphosa (Rom. 16:12) or Euodia and Syntyche (Phil. 4:2). It's almost impossible to decide between these three alternatives, along with much else.

Did Martha and Mary accompany Jesus and the others into Jerusalem as he made his way into the city on a donkey? Did they realise that entering the city mounted in such a way was a symbolic sign and that Jesus was not just any pilgrim, but God's anointed King? Did they shout 'hosanna' with the others, full of excitement and expectation? And did they remember their own private anointing, back home in Bethany with the wider group of disciples, where perhaps Mary took the initiative and anointed Jesus herself?

We're on more stable ground with the story of the Last Supper. Although pilgrims might have stayed on the outskirts of Jerusalem, the Passover meal (known as the *seder*) could only be celebrated in the city itself. This is why the upper room needed to be secured and prepared for the evening. As Jesus' hosts it seems very likely that Martha and Mary would have undertaken the organisation of this task; as locals they would undoubtedly have had contacts in Jerusalem with rooms large enough for their gatherings and they would presumably have made their own arrangements for Passover meals in previous years.

Mark's Gospel (14:12–16) preserves a story in which two unnamed disciples asked Jesus where they should prepare the meal. Jesus, it seems, had already made arrangements and directed the disciples to the place (they were to follow a man with a water jar to find it). It's clear that these two disciples weren't part of the Twelve, as Jesus came to the room later that evening bringing the Twelve with him.

The Greek here refers to these two unnamed disciples in the masculine form, but there's no reason to suppose that they *both* were men (Greek, as we've already seen, automatically assigns masculine gender to groups, even if only one male is present). Whether the sisters or Jesus arranged the room, it's a strong possibility that one of the unnamed disciples here is to be identified as either Martha or Mary, along with an unnamed male disciple (Lazarus?).

And we can be quite sure that these women would have shared the Passover with the men that evening. As hosts and friends of Jesus, it would be inconceivable that Jesus should celebrate a feast that was above all a family gathering in which the whole household should be together at the table without them there. The

Apostolic Church Order, a third-century text from an eastern setting such as Egypt, Asia Minor or Syria, remembers the sisters at the Last Supper. Although the text itself uses the women as mouthpieces to oppose women presiding at the Eucharist, it indirectly supports the view that some in the early church appealed to the sisters' presence there to justify women's ministry. In the Gnostic text known as the *Pistis Sophia*, also from the third century, various disciples who questioned Jesus, probably in a meal context, were Peter, Andrew, John, James, Philip, Thomas, Matthew, Bartholomew, Mary Magdalene, Martha, Salome and Mary the mother of Jesus.

Diverse branches of the early church clearly remembered the two sisters as important disciples. There are good reasons, then, to assume that Martha and Mary – and no doubt other female disciples – were at the first Eucharist, and that they continued to break bread in their home later on. (Is this why Martha is remembered particularly in the context of table service?)

What, though, did the sisters think as the talk turned to Jesus' imminent death? Had they already begun to suspect that this might be the outcome? And what of Jesus' announcement that one of his disciples would betray him? Even if it was clearly one of the Twelve, did the sisters join with the others in searching their souls and asking, 'Could it possibly be me?'

Although no Gospel specifically names them at the cross (unless Mary is to be identified as Mary Magdalene), it is difficult not to imagine that they would have accompanied the other women there, as Orthodox tradition maintains. With their hopes and dreams dashed, did they stay by their Lord until the end? And when it was all over, did they return to the house in Bethany with the other women, only to return to anoint the body on the Sunday morning in a group (as in Luke)? Or was the situation too precarious for people known to have associated with a criminal, and did they need to disappear? We know that Paul rounded up disciples of Jesus later on, both men and women. Although the Gospels are silent on this point, it is not impossible that the sisters were forced to flee from their home in earlier reprisals – the story of a successful transfer to France may obscure a less happy tale.

Empty tomb traditions

It's common among some scholars to argue that the story of the finding of the empty tomb by women early on the Sunday morning is a late tradition with no basis in fact. The apostle Paul never mentions an empty tomb, or women witnesses; neither does the tomb feature in the early speeches in Acts. In both cases, what convinces people of the resurrection are appearances of the risen Jesus, not accounts of an empty grave. The first we hear of the empty tomb is in Mark's Gospel, usually dated to the 70s CE, in an account that was invented – so the argument goes – to underscore the reality of Jesus' risen body.

An empty grave, of course, tells us nothing about how it became that way: the body might have been stolen (by friends or enemies), or simply relocated (as Mary Magdalene assumed in John 20). First-century Jews associated resurrection with the end of time, when God would raise people for judgement. It would hardly be the first thing that people thought of if they heard that a body had disappeared.

More likely, the story of the women's visit to the grave once the Sabbath had passed is a very old one. Women in most ancient societies were associated with mourning, and it would be no surprise to find a group of female disciples returning to a graveside to grieve for their leader. (These women had been hailed as sisters of Jesus, after all, closer than blood relatives.)

Jesus' burial may well have been quick and rudimentary, with none of the usual trappings extended to non-violent deaths – anointing, funeral processions, wailing and so on. But this doesn't mean that his female disciples wouldn't have wanted to show their devotion to his memory by congregating at his grave. It may well have been in this setting, as women shared their stories of Jesus and what he had meant to them, that we have the beginnings of the gospel, the good news of Jesus that would be preached around the Mediterranean. Drawing on their rich scriptural tradition, particularly the deep expressions of grief in the psalms, these women's laments may stand at the very beginning of Christian proclamation.

As we've already seen, in the second century, Celsus – the well-known opponent of Christianity – identified Martha as a teacher with her own following. He claimed to know of groups of Christians who took their names from both Martha and Mariamme. It could well be that there was a group (or even several groups) of women who took their lead from a woman who, along with her sister, was a close associate of Jesus, a prominent female disciple and someone who was central to the events of that momentous Passover.

7

The Anointing Woman

An 'anointing woman' story of some kind appears in each one of our Gospels in the New Testament, and it finds its way into just about every Jesus film there is. In *Jesus Christ Superstar*, Mary Magdalene, as the anointer, sings a song asking Christ to 'Close your eyes, close your eyes and relax, think of nothing tonight'. It comes across as an act of special devotion and intimacy.

But why do the stories differ? How many women anointed Jesus at different times? Should we combine all the stories into one and assume there was just one anointing that was then retold in different ways? Should we suppose that there were two anointings by the same woman, as John seems to suggest: one that had been done previously (which John 11:2 refers to but does not describe) and one in Bethany (John 12:1-8)? Or were there even more than these two, by different women? And why was Jesus anointed by women at all?

It's important to remember the sequence of our Gospels, in terms of when they were written down. Scholars generally agree that Mark was written first, then Matthew and Luke, and finally John. The authors of Matthew and Luke clearly used Mark, retelling the Markan stories in their own narratives (as we saw with the blood-flow woman). The use of the other Gospels made by the author of John's Gospel has been much debated, but overall it is increasingly agreed that Mark was used, and probably Luke too. John relied on the audience's knowledge of the others.

None of our Gospel authors reproduced their source material word for word. They clearly felt it was their prerogative to add or subtract various details, and to shape the stories by reference to their own alternative memories and their own themes. So, if we are trying to get to our historical women disciples of Jesus and have multiple tellings of the same story, we need to work through the texts forensically.

Let's start by looking at Mark, since Mark came first. We've already noted that Mark tended to hide the women in the story of Jesus, until they suddenly turned up at the cross. As we have seen, it was easy to hide them because in ancient Greek, as in many languages today, a masculine plural form of words could stand for both males and females, or just males. So readers often assume that when in Mark we meet 'disciples' and the word is in the masculine plural form, only male disciples are meant. Even a few male disciples in a room full of women would mean that the masculine plural form would be used, rather than the feminine plural. We need to hunt for these in the places where they don't immediately jump out. For example, when Jesus was accused of eating with 'tax-gatherers and sinners' and 'there were many and they followed him' (2:15), we have to imagine that women were also included among these 'sinners'.

Read in line with what we are told of the women at the cross, Jesus' disciples were actually a mixed group of men and women. On the way to Jerusalem, it is said, 'They were on the road, going up to Jerusalem, and Jesus was walking ahead of them, and they were astonished, but those who followed were afraid' (Mark 10:32). This is an interesting detail. The disciples were astonished that Jesus was driving on ahead, but they were afraid. This language of 'they were afraid' (*ephobounto*) is exactly what Mark uses of the women at the empty tomb. The disciples were afraid of the authorities, but they followed Jesus all the same.

Neither in Matthew nor in Luke do we have a repetition of this mention of the scared disciples. But we can well imagine both men and women feeling very worried indeed, given that Jesus had predicted he was going to Jerusalem to die. In fact, he responded to their fears by taking the Twelve aside (from the rest of the larger group of disciples) and repeating that this was really going to happen: he was going to be delivered to the chief priests and scribes, condemned to death, delivered to the Gentiles

(Roman administration), mocked, spat on, whipped and killed, and then would rise again in three days (Mark 10:32–34). It would have been hard to accept that this was good news.

So, in Mark, the whole group of disciples, men and women (and children), arrived in Jericho, Bethphage and Bethany. At this point, Jesus knew that there was a colt tied up in the village located just by the entrance and sent two of his disciples (male and female?) ahead to fetch it, saying, 'If anyone says to you, "Why are you doing this?" say, "The Lord needs it and will send it back right away"' (Mark 11:1–10). This might indicate prophetic knowledge, but Jesus could also have known because he knew Bethany from previous acquaintance and had disciples there who called him 'Lord'. John's insistence that Jesus loved Lazarus, Martha and Mary implies he knew them well. As we hinted in the last chapter, there's something about Bethany that is not really told in Mark, a kind of prequel to the core narrative of Jesus' mission. Jesus knew Bethany, and people there. He had visited before.

Why is all this important? Because the woman who anointed Jesus in the Gospel of Mark (14:3–12) was in Bethany, but she is unidentified. Jesus, as we saw, came and went between Bethany and Jerusalem, and stayed there 'with the Twelve' (Mark 11:11). Actually, it is very likely that other disciples from Galilee were there as well. Unidentified disciples pop up in the passages that follow. But was the anointing woman one of the women disciples from Galilee, or was she from Bethany?

In the Gospel of John (12:2), Martha served at the dinner, and Lazarus reclined, but it's not clear who hosted. In Mark (14:3) the house belonged to Simon the Leper (a nickname of one cured of a skin disease), not Martha. A 'woman' came with an alabaster jar of pure nard, extremely expensive, broke the jar to open it and poured it on Jesus' head. In response, 'some' grumbled and thought it could have been sold for 300 denarii and the proceeds given to poor people. Jesus defended her and said:

> Leave her alone. Why do you cause trouble for her? She did a good thing to me, because you always have poor people with you,

and whenever you want you can (always) do good things for them,
but you do not always have me. She did what she could. She came
ahead to anoint my body beforehand for burial, Amen, I say to
you that wherever the good news will be proclaimed in the whole
world, what she did will be spoken about in remembrance of her.

It seems ironic that this story is recorded in remembrance of this
woman, but her name is not provided when the host's name is.
But that is consistent with the way Mark hides women disciples,
and women's names, until the cross. The motivations of the
woman herself are not stated, but Jesus defended her action as
indicating incredible insight, confirming what he had been telling
his disciples already: he was going to die.

One thing that is really important for our subject is that the
reaction of 'some' demonstrates that the woman herself was one
of the disciples. This is a story about the disciples and Jesus being
hosted at a dinner in Bethany, and thus 'some' of the disciples
complained that valuable resources for their work of *diakonia* were
being wasted. In Mark, just before heading off to Jerusalem, Jesus
had asked of a wealthy man as a condition of him following him,
'Go and sell everything you own, give it to poor people, and
you'll have treasure in heaven, and come follow me' (Mark 10:21).
So 'some' quite rightly reminded the woman what 'serving' Jesus
should mean, as a disciple. We remember again that these disciples
were both men and women. Viewed from the perspective of a
woman who was trying to serve Jesus by contributing to the
movement, part of that service was clearly in helping the poor.
Perhaps it was even particularly galling for a woman who had
been eking out her own resources in providing for Jesus' mission
to see something squandered.

Jesus defended her by saying that in this case she had done
something exceptional, even prophetic. Pouring oil on the head
evokes all sorts of scriptural echoes linked to the anointing of
kings or prophets. King David was anointed while still a shepherd
by the prophet Samuel, and symbolically set apart as God's chosen
one, or Messiah (1 Sam. 16:13). The word Messiah (*Christos* in
Greek) means 'the anointed one', who is conceptually a king.

Mark's scene, then, gives the anointing a new dimension, suggesting that this unnamed woman recognised Jesus as God's anointed in a private ceremony attended only by the disciples.

Mark interweaves the woman's actions with the plots of the chief priests to do away with Jesus; perceptive readers will see the irony that those who should have been publicly anointing Jesus were plotting his death, leaving their work to be done by a woman. Using characteristic paradoxes and inversions, Mark skilfully connects this anointing with his death. While anointing should take place after death, as part of a burial ritual, this was here done beforehand. Jesus assumed no such careful anointing would be allowed to take place at his burial, when he would have been killed as a troublemaker.

If in Mark we have a reasonably accurate telling of an actual event, one motive for the anointing is implied by the use of nard. Nard was a well-known remedy for headaches, understood to have a calming, relaxing effect (Pliny, *Nat. Hist.* 12:26). Nard massaged into someone's head, when inhaled, would have helped soothe and alleviate pain. We can also remember here that one thing Jesus asked his envoys to do in his name was to heal people by anointing them with oil: 'they anointed many sick people with oil and cured them' (Mark 6:12–13; see also James 5:14). In other words, they had oils to use, despite being sent out with no money, no bread and no second tunic (Mark 6:7–9) on the road. So it's no wonder the disciples knew it was worth 300 denarii. If it were not going to be used to heal people, it could at least have been sold!

As already noted, the anointing story follows on from the statement that the chief priests and scribes were looking for a way to arrest Jesus and kill him in secret for fear that there would be a riot if they were to seize him during the festival (Mark 14:1–2). There's no doubt that the last few days of Jesus' life would have been extremely stressful! Whatever the unnamed woman intended, though (and enabling Jesus to relax at a time of stress would be a very good intention), Jesus took the anointing as an action that only confirmed what he was telling everyone would happen: he was going to die.

Was the woman, then, one of those who had come from Galilee, or was she in Bethany already, a disciple of Jesus there (given the colt)? Were the disciples from Galilee saying that she hadn't really got the point of how to use her precious resources? Was she from the household of Simon the Leper? Certainly, it could be that she was Mary, the sister of Lazarus and Martha, and all three siblings were the children of Simon, who had been healed by Jesus. They don't get mentioned in Mark, and Simon doesn't get mentioned in John. Perhaps it's their colt that Jesus borrowed, and he loved them all. But we just can't know.

In Matthew's story of the anointing woman in Bethany (Matt. 26:6–13), the core of Mark is replicated, but with omissions and changes. The event took place in the house of Simon the Leper and a woman came with an alabaster jar. There is no mention of the detail that the perfume was pure nard or that she broke the jar to open it. The precise amount of 300 denarii became 'a lot' of money. But most significantly it was not 'some' of those with Jesus having dinner who complained about her action but 'the disciples'. In other words, the woman was now *outside* the band of disciples. It is an 'us disciples and her' situation.

This is actually consistent with what is done elsewhere in Matthew: the definitive disciples are only the Twelve, defined as twelve named men, and they are presented in a much more favourable light than in Mark. So, in this passage, they didn't 'grumble', which is a rather negative word to apply to them. Jesus didn't say, 'Leave her alone', in a snappy way. There is no mention of 'you' giving to poor people whenever you want or that 'she has done what she could' as if she was showing up their inadequate thinking.

Overall, it doesn't look as if Matthew is using any alternative memories, but only editing Mark. However, when we come to Luke's anointing woman (7:36–50), the 'sinner', much of the story is significantly different. For a start, it did not take place in Bethany. The setting of the story is in the narrative of the Galilean mission. The house belonged to a 'Simon', but he was not identified as a (former) Leper but as a Pharisee. There were no disciples, but rather those reclining with Jesus were others who said in the end, 'Who is this who even remits sins?'

A woman came in who was a 'sinner' of the 'city'. Which 'city'? As we have seen, Jesus in Galilee is not shown as going to cities, but to villages and towns. A Pharisee, a legal scholar, would normally be resident in Jerusalem. At any rate, she was clearly not a disciple, and she came into the dinner with an alabaster jar of perfume, wept at Jesus' feet as he reclined, wet his feet with tears, kissed them, anointed them with perfume and then wiped them with her loosened hair. The Pharisee thought that if Jesus were a prophet he would know that this woman was a sinner. Jesus told a story about repentance, and noted how much more loving she was than his host. Then he said to the woman, 'Your sins have been remitted', and, 'Your faith has saved you. Go in peace.'

We've seen in relation to the women on the road with Jesus how Luke takes something from Mark (the women at the cross, in Jerusalem) and places it back in the story of Galilee, so the author of Luke is not averse to resituating stories found in Mark. As with the women on the road story, another source has been woven in, to create a kind of composite of two different strands of memory. The story of the anointing woman in Mark has an alternative memory woven in, with the common elements being a dinner and a devoted woman who touched Jesus in an honorific way.

Once the elements taken from Mark are extracted, the woman is not actually someone who anointed Jesus' head, but someone who wept at his feet, wet them with her tears and dried them with her loose hair. She was a penitent sinner, not a disciple. She did not anoint Jesus for burial, but showed her grief and need for repentance.

Something terrible had happened to her, in that she had loose hair at a time when all women would have their hair bound up. It would have taken her time to untie her hair from being in a bun, under a hairnet or scarf, and this reveals something significant about her. Unbound, loose hair in Judaea, as in the wider Mediterranean world, was associated with intense grief, not with wayward morals. Her loose hair and her tears were two sides of the same coin: she was deeply sad and emotional.

Women's hairstyles

As with clothes, hairstyles in the early imperial period indicated a great deal about a woman's status and role in society. Wealthy women spent a huge amount of time on their hair – indeed, having the leisure to have one's hair styled was a sign of status. Well-to-do women might have spent several hours with one or even two slaves dressing their hair. It was often curled with hot irons, braided and tied in a bun (sometimes with the addition of a hair piece), sewn into position with blunt needles, waxed, and finished off with a decorative pin.

In the early part of the first century, styles were fairly simple. Fashions were set by the Emperor's household, who favoured neat buns. Towards the end of the first century, however, under the new Flavian dynasty, hairstyles became hugely elaborate, with unnaturally high mounds of curls at the front and a braided bun at the back. It is probably these styles that the (unknown) author of 1 Timothy 2:9 warns against.

Dying hair was popular, especially with henna, which created a reddish tint. People also liked to lighten their hair or cover up the grey. For black hair, Pliny the Elder recommended using leeches left to rot in red wine. (Herod the Great is said to have dyed his hair black to make himself look younger.)

Lower down the social scale, women might still have aimed to dress their hair in fashionable ways, but lack of leisure time meant that styles would be much more natural. Brides, of course, would spend time on their hair, often braiding it with flowers. Loose, flowing hair was associated with mourning and funerals, or young girls.

In the eyes of the Pharisees, her reputation meant that Jesus shouldn't allow himself to be touched by her; most likely they considered her unclean (much like the woman with the blood-flow). But this is fundamentally a story about repentance and forgiveness.

So, actually, we do have two original stories of women touching Jesus at dinner events, one with bound hair, touching Jesus' head (in Mark), and another with unbound hair, weeping at his feet (in an unknown source). It's no wonder really that in Luke they are mashed together, but that reduces the number of women we have who engaged with Jesus in some way by taking the initiative and touching him. Amazingly, in total there are three of these: the blood-flow woman, the anointer of Bethany and this repentant sinner in the house of the Pharisee.

As with the anointer in Bethany, the sinner with unbound hair is quite a mystery. Why should she even have been in the house of the Pharisee? Was she a member of the household who had been accused of wrongdoing? Or did she just burst in from the street? Did she become a disciple of Jesus after this? Did she join the others on the road?

Whatever the case, Luke's synthesis of the two sources needs to be carefully distinguished from what we have in Mark and Matthew, because in Luke it is the story of foot-washing with tears that is key.

When we look back at the Gospel of John, then, we can see how we have the next stage in a synthetic development. From Mark we have the location of Bethany. But Luke is also in view: Mary is even introduced as the very woman who had carried out the action of 'having anointed the Lord with perfume and wiped his feet with her hair' (John 11:2). At this point the audience was meant to remember that Luke had the story of Martha and Mary, who lived in a certain village (Luke 10:38–40). Mary was there, sitting at Jesus' feet, and Martha was distracted 'by much serving'. Here in John, Martha serves, and Mary, rather than sitting at Jesus' feet, was anointing his feet.

The Lukan version seems more strongly represented overall in John, though the alabaster jar is omitted in favour of a unit of weight, a litra (pound). There were no kisses or tears, and no explanation is given for Mary having loose hair, and frankly the loose hair of a mourner is inappropriate. The dinner seems quite celebratory, since Lazarus had been raised.

Mention of pure nard is taken from Mark, but nard applied to Jesus' feet is truly a waste, because nard's calming and headache-curing properties would only have been effective on Jesus' head, when inhaled. So the motive of the woman wasn't at all about soothing; it was about something else. It is stated that the house was full of 'the fragrance of the perfume', which recalls what is found in the Greek version of the Song of Songs 1:3: 'the fragrance of your perfumes is better than all the *aromata*; your name is perfume poured out'.

As elsewhere in the Gospel of John, there is powerful symbolism at work here, drawing on the Song of Songs, and this will return in the scene of Mary witnessing Jesus at the empty tomb, as Hippolytus rightly picked up and developed in his poetic retelling of the resurrection story. The objections of the other disciples are boiled down to a focus only on Judas. The selling price of 300 denarii is given. But Judas is identified as a thief and betrayer (which we know already from Mark and Luke).

In John, Jesus stated of Mary and the perfume, 'Leave her alone, so that she preserves it for the day of my burial. You always have the poor with you, but you do not have me.' This is quite like Mark, but there are changes. While she is described as anointing Jesus, she's now asked to keep the perfume. Jesus did not proclaim Mary as someone whose story would always be told in remembrance of her. She had not, with foresight, anointed him ahead of his burial, but was told to save it. Yet, in John it was Nicodemus and Joseph of Arimathea who supplied this perfume, in an amount a hundred times what Mary had (see John 19:39). She was told to save something she couldn't use.

To summarise here, from the four different ways that the anointing woman story is told in the Gospels, the patterns of influence are most straightforwardly traced by seeing Mark's telling as foundational, with Luke blending this with an alternative story of a repentant woman coming in and grieving at Jesus' feet. John uses Mark and Luke to create another fusion story, with further additions, which may too preserve genuine memories, like the names of the Bethany family. (The relationships are mapped out in the flow chart.)

There is a level one of memory, preserved in Mark and in a source that was used in Luke, then there is a level two in which the story is retold in Matthew and Luke. Finally, there is a level three in which the story is retold again in John. At each point, decisions are made about what to include. The component parts are always malleable.

Level One

Mark	Luke's source
Bethany house of Simon the Leper Jesus reclined (at dinner) a woman an alabaster jar of perfume costly pure nard broke jar poured it on his head some grumbled sold for more than 300 denarii?	city house of Pharisee Jesus lay (at dinner) a woman sinner stood at his feet, weeping, wet his feet with tears wiped them with her hair kissed his feet

Level Two

Matthew 26:6–13	Luke 7:36–50
Bethany house of Simon the Leper Jesus reclined (at dinner) a woman an alabaster jar of perfume very costly poured it on his head disciples indignant could have been sold for a lot	*city* *house of Pharisee* Simon Jesus lay/reclined (at dinner) a woman *sinner in the city* an alabaster jar of perfume *stood at his feet, weeping* *wet his feet with tears,* *wiped them with her hair,* *kissed his feet* an anointed them with perfume + Luke 10:38–42 a certain village Martha served Mary (Mariam) sat at Jesus' feet

Level Three

John 11:2; 12:1–8	Independent story/stories?
Bethany, where Lazarus was they made a dinner *Martha served* Lazarus among those was lying (at dinner) with him *Mary* (Mariam) took a litra (pound) of costly perfume of pure nard *anointed Jesus' feet* *wiped his feet with her hair,* the house was filled with the scent of perfume Judas, one of the disciples, said why was perfume not sold for 300 denarii	Lazarus? Mary? litra (pound)? house filled with scent of perfume? Judas?

The tearful sinner and the anointing woman were not the same person, but they both touched Jesus (feet and head respectively), taking an initiative that is quite surprising. The anointer was a disciple, and the weeper may have become one. In the retellings of the stories, though, we see strategies at work in our texts to blend and re-form them. We do not get inside the original anointing women's heads, as we do with the blood-flow woman; they are always observed by others. We do not have their voices, or their names. Yet they are also shown as being more exemplary than any of the male interlocutors around them. The core lesson seems to be: take your cue from what the women do.

8

Mary the Mother of Jesus

Unlike many of the almost forgotten women in this book, the mother of Jesus has enjoyed a rich and widespread memory. Declared the *Theotokos* (Mother of God) at the Council of Ephesus in 431 CE, she's frequently designated as the Blessed Virgin Mary, the Queen of Heaven, the Madonna or a New Eve. Her legacy has been particularly strong in Roman Catholic and Orthodox circles, where she's believed to have been conceived 'immaculately' (that is, without the stain of original sin) and to have been taken up into heaven at the end of her life, where she now intercedes for those who pray to her. Over the centuries, countless festivals, devotions and prayers have been offered to her, particularly in May and October, and visions of the Blessed Virgin have been widespread (often resulting in pilgrimage sites, such as Lourdes or Guadalupe).

In Christian art, Mary often wears a blue cloak, the colour of the heavens, and is represented in two favourite poses: in scenes of the crucifixion she is the *Stabat Mater* (Latin for 'the mother was standing'), standing by the cross (usually to the right), pale and drawn as she watches her son's torment; and in the *Pietà* (Italian for 'pity' or 'compassion') she tenderly cradles the body of her dead son, now cut down from the cross. While this latter scene isn't based on any specific Gospel passage, it underscores Mary's maternal link to Jesus, and the human tragedy that lies at the origin of Christianity.

Much of what we think we know about Mary comes not from the New Testament itself but from the mid–late second-century text known as the *Protevangelium of James*, which we encountered before when we thought about Salome. The work is a prequel to the Gospels, telling of Mary's own miraculous birth to her well-to-do parents Anna and Joachim, her childhood as a dedicated virgin in the Jerusalem Temple, and the circumstances of her marriage to Joseph. Drawing on a variety of scriptural passages (especially from the story of Samuel), Mary's virginity and purity are praised throughout. As a child, she ate food from the hand of an angel and wasn't 'tainted' by normal bodily functions. Her husband Joseph was a much older man with children from a previous marriage (implying that Jesus' Gospel siblings were step-brothers and sisters). Mary herself was entirely obedient, subordinate and passive – even during labour when Jesus seems miraculously to have appeared from a cloud and light. When Salome asked to subject Mary to an internal examination and touched her (still intact!) hymen, the point was to stress Mary's perpetual virginity, which even childbirth couldn't overcome.

The *Protevangelium* was written at a time when new converts were coming from the pagan world, bringing their assumptions about virgin and/or mother goddesses with them. It's not surprising, then, to find that Mary quickly took on the characteristics of these goddesses – the Great Mother Cybele, the virgin mother Isis and her son Horus (often referred to as the Queen of Heaven and depicted with the child on her lap), and later on the Roman empress. For pagans, the figure of Mary was ready to step into a gap left by the elimination of the female goddesses in the religion of Israel. Presumably women focused on different aspects of Mary and her story at different times in their lives, finding in her a feminine and human face to a more transcendent God.

Yet the cult of Mary has not been without its detractors, with many modern women finding the impossible ideal that she represents – the obedient, passive virgin *and* mother – to be a way of controlling and repressing women.

But what can we say about the woman behind all of this? What was her relationship to her son and the movement that he inaugurated? Strangely, perhaps, Mary does not appear much in the New Testament (she's actually mentioned more frequently in the Quran than in the earliest Christian texts). Paul mentions her only obliquely in Galatians 4:4 (Jesus was 'born of a woman'), and she appears in a couple of passages in the Gospels of Mark and John, and once briefly in Acts 1:14. Her starring role comes in the stories of Jesus' birth found in the Gospels of Matthew and Luke, though only in the latter account does she move to centre stage.

Given Mary's association with the very beginnings of Jesus' story, readers may wonder why we've left her treatment so late in this book. There are broadly two reasons for considering Mary here. First, as we'll see, there are significant difficulties with accepting the birth narratives as historical accounts. And second, the evidence we have may suggest that Mary was more involved with her son's ministry towards its end, and perhaps into the earliest years of the Jerusalem church.

St Issac's Cathedral, Tikhvin Icon of the Theotokos and Infant Jesus

Mary and the birth of Jesus

Although it is retold every Christmas by countless junior school productions (and is by far the best-known part of the Jesus story), it can come as a surprise to realise that Jesus' birth is recounted in only two Gospels – and those accounts are significantly different! In Matthew, Jesus is presented as a second Moses, drawing not only on traditions in Exodus 1–2 but also on a wealth of later Jewish ideas associated with the patriarch. The story focuses on Jesus' father, Joseph, who was initially hesitant to marry Mary because she was found to be pregnant (in the Moses story the early hesitation was because Pharoah had decreed that Israelite babies were to be killed). Reassured through a dream, Joseph did take Mary as his wife and Jesus was born. Another dream, however, warned him of Herod's evil plot (modelled again on Pharoah's murderous edict), and the holy family escaped to Egypt and later settled in Galilee. Thus, Matthew explains how Jesus came to be born in Bethlehem (the city of David) but grew up in Nazareth.

The account in Luke's Gospel is rather different. The whole of Luke 1–2 presents us with an elaborate parallel between the births of John the Baptist and Jesus, showing at every turn that the circumstances of Jesus' birth were more miraculous than those of his forerunner. So if John was born to an old, barren couple, Jesus was born to a virgin who had not yet known a man. And if John's birth was accompanied by the strange events surrounding his name, Jesus was visited not only by local shepherds but also by an angelic throng. In Luke's Gospel, the family home was always in Nazareth, and it was because of a Roman census that the holy family found themselves in Joseph's ancestral village of Bethlehem for the birth of their son. The whole account is peppered with Lukan concerns: it presents the holy family as poor (they could only offer two doves in the Temple), it shows an interest in society's marginalised (Jesus was visited by shepherds rather than foreign astrologers), and it demonstrates that events on the world stage (the census) inadvertently helped to promote the Christian message.

Despite their differences, however, the two accounts agree that Jesus' parents were named Mary and Joseph, that he was born in Bethlehem and that there was something unusual about the way in which Mary conceived. Luke is very clear that this took place while she was still a virgin (Luke 1:34). Matthew is less explicit in the narrative itself (1:18 only mentions a child 'by the Holy Spirit'), but includes a quotation from Isaiah 7:14 which says that a *parthenos* will conceive (Matt. 1:23). The Greek word *parthenos* can simply refer to a young woman of marriageable age, though this wouldn't have much significance in the context – all that the author of Matthew's Gospel would be saying is that Mary was the girl that Isaiah had in mind all those years earlier. More likely, Matthew does want to suggest that there was something miraculous about Jesus' birth, and that his mother conceived while still a virgin.

The fact that this tradition is found in both Gospels (though in rather different ways) suggests that it predates both of them. But what are we to make of it? And what does it say about Mary?

From the mid-second century, an alternative tradition claimed that Mary was an adulteress and that Jesus was illegitimate. The pagan philosopher Celsus argued that Jesus' mother was a poor Jewish woman who earned her living by spinning. She was convicted of adultery with a Roman soldier named Panthera and thrown out of her husband's house (Origen, *Against Celsus* 1:32). The charge of illegitimacy surfaced again in Rabbinic sources, and much later in a medieval Jewish life of Jesus known as the *Toledot Yeshu*. The question is, of course, which came first? Did rumours of Jesus' illegitimacy lead to Christian counterclaims that Mary conceived while still a virgin, or did the Christian story of Mary's virginal conception lead detractors to charge her with adultery?

Some have seen faint echoes of Jesus' illegitimacy in the New Testament itself. In Mark 6:3, the villagers of Nazareth referred to Jesus as the 'son of Mary', and in John 8:41 Jesus' opponents said to him, '*We* are not illegitimate children' (perhaps implying that Jesus was). Neither of these is conclusive, however. While it is certainly unusual for a son to be known by his mother's name, it would make some sense if Joseph had been dead a long time. And the opponents in John were talking about being legitimate children of Abraham in a characteristically symbolic passage from which it would be unwise to look for historical information. In John elsewhere Jesus is clearly called 'son of Joseph' (John 1:45), and the Nazareth villagers said, 'Is this not Jesus son of Joseph, whose father and mother we know?' (John 6:42; see also Luke 4:22).

All in all, it seems more likely that Christian claims for Jesus' virginal conception gave rise to counter-charges of illegitimacy.

Biographers of great heroes like Alexander the Great liked to give their subjects extraordinary births, and we can easily imagine that those who created these early traditions wanted to go beyond the scriptural stories of conceptions by barren or elderly parents. Jesus' conception has certain similarities with that of the Emperor Augustus, whose mother Atia encountered a serpent in a dream at the Temple of Apollo and later found she was pregnant. Such stories underlined not only the greatness of the subject, but in a Jewish context showed that Jesus was chosen for God's purposes from the very moment of his miraculous conception.

In the end, none of this tells us very much at all about Mary and her relationship with Joseph and her son. We've already seen that family life was complex in this period, with life expectancy short and sudden death common. We shouldn't think in terms of an either/or here: either the traditional nuclear family of Christmas cards or a dysfunctional single-parent arrangement brought on by pregnancy outside marriage. It's quite possible that Mary was pregnant before her marriage – such was commonplace in most societies even into the modern period; what mattered for legitimacy (and the avoidance of shame) was that the couple were married before the child was born.

It's also quite likely that Mary was desperately young by our standards at her first marriage, and that Joseph was quite a lot older. If he died, Mary may have married again, perhaps more than once (step-siblings would be very common, and we can't be sure that all the brothers and sisters referred to in the Gospels shared a father with Jesus). Or perhaps Mary remained on her own, trusting to the support of her now grown-up sons and wider family. Any of these scenarios would be perfectly normal and accepted within first-century Galilean society.

Our only story relating to Jesus' childhood comes from Luke's Gospel (Luke 2:41–51). Every year, we're told, the family went to Jerusalem to celebrate the Passover. One year, however, when Jesus was twelve years old (the age of manhood), his parents realised after a day's travel homewards that their son wasn't with them. After searching for three days, they found him in the Temple, in earnest discussion with the teachers and amazing all who heard him. Unsurprisingly, Mary was annoyed at her son (who seemed to have no awareness of the trouble he'd caused): 'Child, why have you treated us like this?' she says. 'Look, your father and I have been searching for you in great anxiety.' But Jesus seemed taken aback, saying, 'Did you not know that I must be in my Father's house?'

Stories like this are commonly found in biographies of great teachers. The purpose is to suggest that Jesus' remarkable abilities were already apparent even as a young man. (The historian Josephus tells a similar story about his own prodigious learning as a child.) We would be wise therefore not to set too much historical store by the story's main themes. And yet, behind the stereotypical motifs, the anecdote may connect with memories of a pious family that did make the yearly pilgrimage to Jerusalem for the Passover, travelling with a large company of friends and neighbours (rather like the company that Jesus would surround himself with later on). And perhaps, too, we can hear echoes of devoted parents who would search any number of days for their missing son.

The comment that Mary 'treasured all these things in her heart' is part of the author's recurring note that Jesus' mother mulled over all these surprising events, trying to work out what it might all mean (almost the same phrase occurs earlier, after Jesus' birth, in 2:19). Yet the phrase may well have some historical basis. Maybe Mary was surprised and initially delighted by her son's piety and understanding; maybe she found in him a kindred spirit with whom she could talk about her love for God and their shared Jewish faith.

Luke's Gospel gives Mary a psalm of praise to sing in 1:46–55 (usually referred to as the *Magnificat*), delighting in God's care for the weak and powerless and God's ongoing promises. Filled with the Holy Spirit she acted as a prophet, like her namesake Miriam, the sister of Moses. (The name *Miriam* was written as *Mariam* in Greek; interestingly, the author of this passage refers to Mary – who is usually known as *Maria* – as *Mariam* in 1:30, perhaps deliberately alluding to the earlier prophet.)

Jesus may have learnt much from his mother. Perhaps he sat on her knee while she recounted the stories of Israel. Perhaps she instilled in him a strong sense of fairness. Was it Mary who first taught him to consider the lilies of the field and the birds of the air? And was Mary herself a gifted storyteller?

Since Joseph (or any other stepfather) is not found alive in Jesus' adult ministry, it seems quite likely that Mary was a widow and that the tradition that she did not remarry is sound. A widow was only valuable as a bride if she was considered to have a good number of child-bearing years ahead of her, and child-bearing age in antiquity, as in many deprived parts of the world today where nutrition is poor, could be over quite early.

In Jesus' parables and teaching, widows were often identified as vulnerable and poor. While actually we know there could be some wealthy widows in antiquity, this characterisation of widows in Jesus' teaching is striking. Jesus noted the great giving of a poor widow in the Jerusalem Temple, whose two small coins were all she had (Mark 12:41–44). Pharisees were roundly told off for 'devouring' widows' houses (Matt. 23:14). Jesus was filled with pity at the death of the only son of a widow in Nain, perhaps recognising that not only had she lost her only child but that also her security depended on having the son to work and look after her (Luke 7:11–17).

The strength of Jesus' ties with his heavenly Father shouldn't lead us to underestimate the impact of his mother on his formative years. But what about Jesus' ministry? There's evidence to suggest that Mary was not a supporter of her son's activities, at least in its earliest stages.

Mary and Jesus' ministry

John's Gospel places Jesus' mother (who is never named) at his very first miracle when he turned water into wine at the marriage at Cana (John 2:1–11). Mary was a guest at the wedding, along with Jesus and his disciples, when the unthinkable happened – the wine ran out! The bride's family were at risk of social embarrassment and disgrace. Mary showed an extraordinary belief that her son could do something about the situation and went to him with her concerns. Jesus himself, however, was less keen to intervene and seemed to act rather churlishly towards his mother. 'Woman, what concern is that to you and to me?' he said, noting rather enigmatically that his 'hour has not yet come'. And yet Mary advised the servants to do whatever Jesus commanded, confident that her son would save the day – which, of course, he did.

It's difficult to know what to make of this scene. Not only is it unique to John's Gospel, but it's also full of symbolism. The mention of Jesus' 'hour' refers to his death, and the scene in some ways anticipates Jesus' crucifixion (where, in this Gospel, Jesus' mother would appear again). An abundance of good wine is commonly associated with a great banquet at the end when God will gather the faithful, and clearly the author of this passage wants to show that this golden age had now arrived.

What's unclear is whether Mary already had some sense of Jesus' destiny, or whether she was simply a mother trying to do something to help a difficult situation. John tends to be positive towards women, often holding them up as paragons of discipleship (as we saw earlier in the discussion of Martha and Mary). But Mary made no special confession of faith here, unlike Nathanael who had already declared Jesus to be the 'Son of God' and 'King of Israel' (John 1:49). All Mary showed is a confidence that her boy could do something to help.

Mark's Gospel is less positive towards Mary. Here we read of an incident in which Jesus went 'home' (to Capernaum) after going up to the mountain to appoint the Twelve, and a huge crowd gathered, pressing him on all sides to heal the sick and distressed. The scene was inside a house, probably the house of Peter. Jesus was kept so busy that he didn't have time to eat, and people were saying that he had 'gone out of his mind' (Mark 3:19–21).

Jesus' mother and siblings arrived, ready to 'restrain him'. Presumably they were worried for him, thinking he had over-exerted himself and needed to come home and rest. When Jesus heard that they were standing outside, however, he asked, 'Who are my mother and my siblings?' (Mark 3:31–35). Looking at the assembled people in the house, he reinterpreted what it meant to be his family. It's no longer biological kinship that matters, he declared, but faith in him. His true family are those who sit around him and pay attention to his words: 'Whoever does the will of God is my brother and sister and mother.'

This is all good news for Jesus' 'sisters' – those women who came to him (perhaps for healing) and stayed to listen to his message. We've met such women several times already in this book. But the story is hard on Mary and her children, who are disparaged and ignored, replaced by strangers and left 'outside' (always a bad place to be in Mark).

If there was any doubt about the negative labelling of Jesus' biological family here, it's dispelled by the presence of 'scribes from Jerusalem' whose claims that Jesus was demon possessed are interwoven with the concerns of his family. Readers are encouraged to read both these stories together, to make connections between the overtly hostile accusation of the scribes and the actions of his family – however well intentioned. Both groups, in the end, threaten Jesus' ministry.

Later on in this Gospel, Jesus went back to his home town of Nazareth and preached in the synagogue there (Mark 6:1–6). Although entranced by his teaching at first, the townspeople quickly took offence because they knew him: 'Is not this the carpenter, the son of Mary and brother of James and Joses and Judas and Simon, and are not his sisters here with us?' He was just one of them, they thought, and yet here he was giving himself airs and graces.

Interestingly, although Mary and her sons were named, the family made no appearance in this story. It's hard to avoid the impression that they had snubbed Jesus, perhaps with his harsh words from earlier still ringing in their ears. If so, that would add a particular sadness to Jesus' proverbial comment that 'Prophets are not without honour, except in their home town, and *among their own kin*, and in their own house.' (When Matthew and Luke rewrote this they omitted the phrase in italics, presumably because their birth stories – and the passage of time – required a rather more favourable portrait of Jesus' relationship with his family.)

John's Gospel also preserves a tradition that Jesus' siblings weren't followers (John 7:5). And perhaps most curious of all is a short exchange in Luke's Gospel (which is otherwise positive towards Mary): in Luke 11:27–28, a woman in the crowd shouted out, 'Blessed is the womb that bore you and the breasts that nursed you!' Jesus, however, in a manner reminiscent of Mark 3, said, 'Blessed rather are those who hear the word of God and obey it!'

In Jesus' teaching there is a clear sense that he and his disciples would experience conflict with their families in exchange for their obedience to God. Families could appeal to traditional values and family love to curb any enthusiasm for Jesus and his message, and ask people to come back home. Jesus responded, 'Anyone loving father or mother more than me is not worthy of me and anyone loving son or daughter more than me is not worthy of me. And the one who does not take their cross and follow me is not worthy of me' (Matt. 10:37; see also Luke 14:26). And again, 'Do not suppose that I have come to bring peace to the earth. It is not peace I have come to bring but a sword. For I have come to set son against father, daughter against mother, daughter-in-law against mother-in-law. A person's enemies will be the members of their own household' (Matt. 10:34–36; Luke 12:51–53 adds 'mother against daughter and daughter against mother'). These kinds of statements are also found in the *Gospel of Thomas* (16, 101).

What's clear in all these is that there is quite a gender balance, and this teaching is intended to emphasise the cost of discipleship. For the Gospel writers, showing Jesus as having family troubles provides the readers with a model. He himself stood firm when his own family wanted to take him home.

Nevertheless, it's hard to see why Jesus' earliest followers would circulate unflattering traditions about his family unless they had some basis in historical fact. Perhaps behind all of this is a recollection that Jesus' mother and at least some of his family were not supportive of his ministry, at least in its early days. (We've already seen that at least one of Jesus' sisters may have been a follower, perhaps from quite early on, see Chapter 2.)

If Jesus was the eldest son (as is traditionally assumed), Mary might well have depended on him, especially if Joseph was dead, and expected him to provide for the family, to arrange his sisters' marriages and to arrange her own affairs. Instead, Jesus chose to be immersed by John the Baptist and later to strike out in his own ministry as a charismatic healer and teacher throughout the towns and villages of Galilee. While the crowds flocked to Jesus with enthusiasm, those left behind in Nazareth may well have felt abandoned.

Passover in Jerusalem

A cluster of references connected to Jesus' last visit to Jerusalem, however, suggest that this may not be the full picture. Taken individually, they can all be explained away, but together they suggest that Mary and at least some of Jesus' siblings did come to believe in him later in his ministry.

The first thing to note is the clear assertion in John's Gospel that Jesus' mother and her sister were among the women at the foot of the cross (John 19:25–27). This is the only Gospel specifically to mention Mary's presence here, and the whole scene is characteristically symbolic. We're presented with a conversation between Jesus, Mary and a character known as the 'Beloved Disciple' who's presented throughout this Gospel as an idealised follower, always understanding and bearing witness to the deeper meaning of events (see Chapter 6). Jesus asked them to look after one another in a brief moment, with the newly formed 'mother and son' standing at the heart of the new Christian community that would be founded on the death of Jesus. For John, Jesus' (unnamed) mother bookends his earthly ministry – she acted as midwife to its beginning and a witness to his death.

Just because something is symbolic, of course, doesn't necessarily mean that it can't also be historically accurate. Mark and the other evangelists certainly don't mention Mary's presence at the crucifixion, and it seems unlikely that she would be included among 'many other women' without specific mention. But if the now mature Mary and her family were in Jerusalem for the Passover, she may have hoped for some kind of reconciliation, or to spend time with him (and perhaps his believing sister). When news spread of his arrest and condemnation, she may well have been drawn to Golgotha, whatever hurt and distress she may have felt before. Crucifixion was a deliberately degrading yet public form of execution. It's hard to imagine a mother not standing by her son at his moment of greatest need, channelling his pain into every fibre of her own body. Was it there perhaps that she became a believer?

We have some corroboration for Mary's presence in Jerusalem from the Acts of the Apostles, which puts her and Jesus' siblings in the upper room with the other disciples after the ascension (Acts 1:14). It's possible again that theological interests are uppermost here – there are a number of parallels between events in Luke's Gospel and Acts (designed to show that events turned out according to a divine pattern), and the mention of Mary here at the start of the story of the church is a neat parallel to her appearance in the Gospel at the start of the story of Jesus. But again, the detail may be historical, in which case Mary and Jesus' siblings would likely have been there at Pentecost and played a role at the very beginning of the Christian proclamation (Acts 2:1–4).

A third piece of evidence is the vision of the risen Jesus by his brother James. The author of Acts says very little about James, and his emergence as leader of the Jerusalem community is never explained (he simply took over after Peter fled from Agrippa in Acts 12:17, and later assumed command, 15:13–21, 21:17–18). Undoubtedly, the reason for James' meteoric rise from nowhere was his vision of the risen Jesus, noted by Paul in 1 Corinthians 15:7. It's difficult to know when the vision occurred, but we may plausibly put it sometime in this very early period, most likely in Jerusalem. In the mysterious and missing *Gospel of the Hebrews*, there was apparently a story in which James ate bread with the risen Jesus (Jerome, *On Illustrious Men* 2). Once again, we get a sense of Mary and her family coming to faith during that fateful Passover in Jerusalem.

Finally, it's worth considering one further aspect of the portrait of Mary in the Lukan birth stories. We've already seen that she's cast as a prophet, like Moses' sister Miriam. Perhaps even clearer, however, is her presentation as a disciple. In many respects, she functions as a model believer: she consented to the divine call through the angel Gabriel (Luke 1:38) and persisted in her faithful obedience even though she didn't always understand the implications of what was happening around her. Perhaps this identification of Mary as a disciple derives not so much from the time around Jesus' conception as from a memory of her later belief in and devotion to her son's mission.

Mary's house in Ephesus

In John 19:25–27, Jesus urged his mother and the Beloved Disciple to relate to one another as mother and son. The short episode ends with the note that 'from that hour the disciple took her into his own home'. The Beloved Disciple has traditionally been identified as John Zebedee (who is otherwise often strangely absent in this Gospel).

An early tradition, known to both Irenaeus and Eusebius, claims that after the disciples were persecuted in Jerusalem, John Zebedee took Mary to Ephesus in Turkey (see map on page 150). Based on visions of the German nun and mystic Anne Catherine Emmerich, a tiny house some distance from Ephesus was identified as the place where Mary lived out her earthly life before her assumption. Although there is no evidence that Mary ever went anywhere near Ephesus, the site has become a major place of pilgrimage, particularly for Roman Catholics.

9

Tabitha

Tabitha is not a 'Gospel woman' – she doesn't appear in the Gospels of Matthew, Mark, Luke or John, or other Christian apocryphal Gospels or in early Christian literature as one of the women who followed Jesus. She appears instead in the Acts of the Apostles, where she is specifically called a 'disciple'.

While she is acknowledged as a saint in the Western (Latin) and Eastern Orthodox Churches, her main claim to fame is having been raised from the dead, like Lazarus. She is the recipient of this miraculous action by Peter, after Jesus' death and resurrection. But the fact that the other disciples of Joppa are so determined that she should live gives us an implied backstory to Tabitha. Furthermore, what is said about her helps us understand what Jesus' women disciples focused on in their own types of ministry.

The Acts of the Apostles

Before we go on, let's look at the Acts of the Apostles. This is actually the second instalment of the Gospel of Luke, and we might even talk about the 'Gospel of Luke–Acts'. In this second instalment, the focus is on how the Holy Spirit, sent by Jesus, keeps the movement going and growing through the Mediterranean world and on to Rome.

There's thematic consistency between the Gospel of Luke and the Acts of the Apostles, and both instalments are introduced by the same person, as an 'I', writing to a respected figure called Theophilus. Later on in Acts, this 'I' is actually a player in the narrative, when the work jumps into using 'we' language: the 'we' includes Paul and the 'I' we meet at the start. The 'we-passages' have long been a conundrum (Acts 16:10–17; 20:5–15; 21:1–18; 27:1–28:16). While tradition eventually seized upon Luke as the person behind these passages (Philem. 24; Col. 4:14; 2 Tim 4:11), many scholars today doubt this. We need to remember that Paul could travel with female companions (1 Cor. 9:5), and hailed Euodia and Syntyche as fellow workers (Phil. 4:2), along with Prisca. So, unless we simply adopt the traditional view, any thinking about the identity of the author should take this into account.

If the author was a woman, this may explain why there are quite a few important women who followed Jesus and supported the mission in Acts, and Prisca is mentioned in a very familiar way as 'Priscilla', as if she was known as a friend (see below). But the narrative also keeps the women from too much view and presents the important, driving roles of men, perhaps because the recipient – Theophilus – is much more interested in male role models. There may well have even been some textual editing to ensure that was the case, as we see in later manuscripts, where tweaking continued to occur.

There are big questions that arise about how we might define a 'woman's view' here, and we need to remember that among women themselves there was likely a variety of perspectives about how to be a disciple of Jesus when it came to a strongly gendered society in which patriarchy was simply the norm. How much do you rock the boat, especially when your whole driving ethos has been built around the idea of *diakonia*, 'service', compassion and turning the other cheek? If being self-effacing was what the disciples of Jesus should be about, it was perhaps natural for women to efface themselves. And there were real reasons to downplay themselves. The situation portrayed in the second-century *Acts of Paul and Thecla* indicates that a young Christian woman who refused to marry a pagan husband could be vilified and murdered by her family.

There were various pitfalls in presenting women. They could be seen as guilty of sexual impropriety or stupid, and – by their very presence – critics could ridicule and undermine the church as a whole.

Following the Way

Acts frequently uses the language of philosophy, in which a teacher would have disciples (students) who would learn a particular body of teaching. The disciples would then be able to pass this teaching on to others. In Acts this teaching is called 'the Way' (Acts 9:2; 18:25–26; 19:9, 23; 22:4; 24:14, 22), which was 'the Way of God' that Jesus had revealed (Luke 20:21). In an early Christian manual, the Didache ('the Teaching'), the 'way of life' is called 'the way of the teaching', that is the teaching of Jesus (Did. 2:2, 6:1 cf. 1:1–4:12, Ep. Barnabas 18–20).

The strong likelihood is that we are not going to find perfect female role models, in Luke–Acts or anywhere else, that conform to what we think of as ideals for female emancipation or equality. We need to open our view to think of how these women operated as disciples of Jesus within the constraints of their own time. Overall, in Luke–Acts the author seems to bring in women at critical times to point in the direction of their roles without spelling it all out. In Luke 8:1–3 the women disciples travelled with Jesus and provided for him and the Twelve out of their resources. Luke 10:39 describes Mary sister of Martha sitting at Jesus' feet. As we have seen, this explicitly defines the position of a student sitting at the feet of the teacher, who is sitting down in order to teach, from Socrates who sits at the feet of Diotima to learn her teaching (Plato, *Symposium* 206b), up until today in Cairo University, where in classes on Islamic theology students adopt the same traditional posture of sitting on the floor at the feet of the teacher. These passages simply indicate the inclusion of women in the category of disciples (students) of Jesus as a matter of course.

Luke–Acts in fact indicates full awareness that it was problematic to promote the experiences of women. At the end of the mysterious events that led to the birth of Jesus we are told that Mary stored up all these things in her heart (Luke 2:51, cf. 19), as if telling them would sound crazy. In Luke 24:10, when the women did reveal the events at the empty tomb, there is the stereotype of distrust in women's evidence: 'the eleven (male apostles) and all the others' thought their story was absolute nonsense.

But women were disciples, and part of the mission. Acts mentions that the zealous Saul persecuted those who followed the Way (of God), both men and women (Acts 9:2). Prisca taught; Lydia the businesswoman hosted a house church (Acts 16:40). Women were there, and they had apparently always been there. In Acts, Tabitha just appears as a disciple, and there is nothing particularly exceptional about that. The problem was that she died.

The raising of Tabitha is placed early on in the narrative of Acts, as part of a cycle of stories about Peter that is interrupted by sequences on Philip and Saul/Paul. Within the Peter sequence we learn a lesson about how a couple (of disciples) named Ananias and Sapphira acted in terms of their resources (Acts 5:1–11). They sold some property and laid the proceeds at the apostles' feet. This shows what was expected: giving everything to the work of the community, for the sake of the kingdom. But Ananias and Sapphira were disingenuous in their actions, because they held some of the proceeds back for themselves and lied, and when Peter challenged them on this, they 'fell down and died'.

So, to start off, we have this shocking death story – not one that people much like to focus on today! But what it indicates is an equality in terms of Jesus' women disciples, in that both Ananias and Sapphira, together as a couple, bore the same responsibility for their resources and how they would be used. The story creates a template for the practice of disciples in the community (*ekklesia*, church). Men and women together gave over their resources for the common work and support of all.

The author of Luke–Acts is then quite concerned to show how people with resources should behave, whether male or female, as disciples of Jesus. The Holy Spirit demands action. It was not all about belief and trust in Jesus; that trust has to follow through in a radical commitment to living in community (see Acts 2:42–47).

In a story of how the disciples were increasing in number, we learn how the Jerusalem community dealt with an issue of food distribution. They had been sharing food from house to house, eating meals together (Acts 2:46). But things went a bit wrong, because some Greek-speaking widows (as we have seen, divorced as well as bereaved women) were being overlooked in the daily serving of food. In a community where everyone was supposed to share resources, fair distribution was clearly an issue. This seems to have been a responsibility of the Twelve, as men, but they devolve it now to seven others while 'we will devote ourselves to prayer and ministry [*diakonia*] of the teaching' (6:4). This practical side of *diakonia* (equal distribution of food serving) put into practice what is said in the Lord's prayer – 'give us today our daily bread' – but clearly *diakonia* was a very broad thing.

This story shows that part of what the Twelve were expected to do as Jesus' envoys was to serve the community by distributing food to everyone (the usual role of women and slaves); but now, with this upset, the Twelve thought this part of their role should be cut out and given to others as their primary responsibility. In a way, it is a 'first becoming last' story, in that the role of men would not usually have involved something so menial as serving food, especially to widows. Shouldn't the story be about how the widows were serving food to the men? The whole scenario is topsy turvy in terms of social norms, and it indicates that men were actually to take a *lowly* position while 'full of the Holy Spirit and of wisdom' (6:5). And it also seems to be very specific to the Jerusalem church, part of the phase when the mission was centred on Jerusalem and Judaea.

But the plot thickens, in that the term 'widows' in the early church doesn't just mean divorced or bereaved women who were dependent on the community for support. Being a 'widow' (*chera*) was actually a designated ministry role (see box). The widows had their own *diakonia*, which involved caring for people in the community and teaching women. So, read in this way, the important Greek-speaking widows were not being adequately served with the food they could then use in their work of service. The men were not doing their job, and had to sort themselves out. And so we come to Tabitha.

Being a 'widow'

In the early third century, the Christian scholar Tertullian indicated that widows were counsellors and cared specifically for the women of the church. They were interpreters of prophecy, and they were seated along with the overseers (episkopoi), *elders* (presbyteroi) *and deacons when the church met* (Tertullian, de Pudic. *13:7;* de Virg. Vel. *9:3;* ad Uxorem *1:7:4).*

Likewise, his contemporary Origen understood that widows had a ministerial role in the teaching of young women (Orat. *28:4;* In Joh comm. *32:12), and were themselves elders:* presbutides *and* presbuteris *(Origen,* In Is. Hom *6:3).*

In the Testamentum Domini *(fifth century), widows had oversight over female deacons and other female presbyters in the same way that bishops had oversight over male deacons and presbyters. A widow was chosen, ordained and seated next to the bishop. She taught women, examined female deacons, prayed, anointed the sick (as part of healing) and also anointed women at baptism* (Test. Dom. *1:40).*

The raising of Tabitha

At the start of our story, Peter was busy with his ministry of healing and the Word/teaching, and arrived in Lydda (Lod) to visit the 'holy people' (people who had been baptised and were in possession of the Holy Spirit, i.e. disciples) who lived there. He healed a man named Aeneas. But he was quickly called to Joppa, for Tabitha (9:36–43).

This incident likely took place in the mid-30s CE, not very long after Jesus' death, so it is quite possible that Tabitha did actually know Jesus and had long been a disciple. Perhaps Peter already knew her. Lydda was inland some 10km from Joppa, which was an ancient port and Judaea's traditional gateway to the Mediterranean Sea. The Greeks linked it with the legend of Perseus and Andromeda, and Jews connected it with Jonah (Jonah

1:12). It therefore looked two ways, culturally, and would have been the busy hub of peoples of trades that we find in any port.

We can even visualise something of the house where Tabitha was living, because there are interesting details in this story, in terms of the space. Her body was washed and laid out in a room 'upstairs'. We can think of closely packed two- or three-storey structures in this busy port town.

In Joppa, the disciples, who had heard that Peter was in Lydda, sent two (speedy) men to him with an urgent plea: 'Please come to us without delay.' Peter went off right away. If he knew Tabitha, her death would have been a shock. The promise of healing for those who trusted in Jesus must have led everyone to hope that the world would be transformed and the kingdom would come before any more of the disciples died except by the hands of the authorities.

How could God have let Tabitha die? The challenge would have been as great as when Lazarus had died. There the critics said, 'Couldn't this man, who opened the eyes of someone blind, have kept this man also from dying?' (John 11:37). The holy people of Lydda and Joppa should have been those who were full of the Spirit. Perhaps her fellow disciples had already tried to bring her back to life. If the Holy Spirit brought healing, why did Tabitha die?

Tabitha is introduced by describing her as 'a certain disciple (*mathetria*) named Tabitha, which translated means "Gazelle"' (9:36). Incredibly, we now not only have a woman actually defined as a 'disciple' as well as her name, but also the meaning of her name, as if this is significant. A gazelle was one of the clean animals Jews could eat (Deut. 14:4), but it is more likely that noting her name is intended to say something about her as a character: we may imagine her as light-footed and nimble. Indeed, the description of her name is followed by a statement about what she did (as a disciple): she was 'full of good works and acts of mercy' (Acts 9:36).

Her work, though not specifically called *diakonia*, is really important in terms of her following Jesus, since elsewhere in Acts, Peter states quite precisely that Jesus 'went about doing good' (*euergeton*) (Acts 10:38), like Tabitha. As for the 'acts of mercy' (*elemosynai*) these were also done by Paul, in distributing charity to the needy (Acts 24:17).

There is no indication of Tabitha having a husband; she was either an unmarried virgin or a widow. Her companions were 'holy ones and widows' who were called in by Peter after he raised her (9:41). Actually, the widows were a designated grouping within the 'holy ones' as a whole. In the upper room where her body lay, 'all the widows wept and showed [Peter] the tunics and mantles that [Tabitha], while she was with them, had made' (Acts 9:39). We have a group of widows, and they pointed to the important *diakonia* they were engaged in, and Tabitha's monumental contribution. In other words, showing what Tabitha had done practically, in weaving and sewing these garments herself, showed how she contributed to the virgins' and widows' work in the church.

Within the New Testament, we best get a clue as to widows' work in 1 Timothy, and it is worthwhile looking at this text. What is said about widows is slightly complicated by the statement about married women earlier in the text. In that earlier spot, the author says, 'I do not allow a woman/wife to teach or to dominate over a man/husband, but to be in silence' (1 Tim. 2:12). This appears to be concerned with women who are wives of men, in a mixed learning environment, since we discover that the women concerned are expected to have children, so they are not virgins or widows (2:15).

Still, it is one thing to say that married women (for social propriety reasons) should not teach adult men, and it is another to say that women cannot teach about Jesus *at all* to anyone, which is often how this has been interpreted. However, in an influential early Christian text called *The Shepherd of Hermas*, a woman named Grapte is in charge of teaching the widows and orphans. She was likely a widow herself, who was instructing them in how to fulfil their own roles. *The Shepherd of Hermas* was considered authoritative scripture by many Christians of the fourth century, and is included as such in an important Christian Bible: the Codex Sinaiticus. Since in this codex 1 Timothy is also authoritative scripture, people clearly did not read 1 Timothy as an all-out ban on women teaching.

The widows of 1 Timothy were themselves a significant group complementing the *episkopoi* (overseers, bishops). Here an overseer is thought to have been a mature man, someone who had been married just once (whether this means he only had one wife, or was married once and was no longer, is not clear in the text) and shown to be a competent householder with children, and who was thought well of by people outside the church. Such essential items for his CV implies that an overseer had a householder function in terms of his role in the church, providing hospitality to the community in his home, and it was assumed this was usually going to be a man, since male householders were the usual thing.

However, one may note that this was not always the case. In Acts 12:12 there is Mary, the mother of John Mark, who hosted the community, gathered together praying, and Paul mentions Nympha, who had a church in her house (Col. 4:15). Just as there were special rules about overseers, though, it is insisted in 1 Timothy that someone enrolled as a widow should be over the age of sixty, 'well attested for her *good works*, (known) as a child-rearer, as one with hospitality, as one who washed the feet of the holy ones, as one who helped the afflicted, and devoted herself to *doing good* in every way' (5:9–10).

The language of this letter parallels what we have in the description of Tabitha, in terms of specific *diakonia* appropriate for an enrolled widow. Tabitha fits this model of a disciple who had a particular ministry. It was the women who took on the role of 'widows' and then men, normatively, who took on the role of 'overseers', but there is no reason to think one role was superior to the other. In fact, in 1 Timothy, the widows were to be exceedingly Christlike, in washing the feet of the holy ones: we think of the model of Jesus washing the feet of his disciples in John 13:1–20. Again, paradoxically, a menial service is elevated to an indicator of superiority in the church.

There are clearly worries in 1 Timothy about perceived social propriety among the widows, because it was bad news for young women to fall for someone and get married when they had actually vowed to be celibate. It was also bad news for them to be too chatty when they went from house to house (with their *diakonia*). The writer didn't like to think of young women gossiping! Instead, in 1 Timothy the widows were expected to continue in supplications and prayers night and day (5:5). It is also not indicated in either case what the full job descriptions of the overseers and widows might have been; there was simply a concern – in both cases – to limit the roles to those who were suitably qualified and reputable in terms of the morals of wider society. The concern in the pastoral epistles is with decent behaviour, and that both overseers/bishops and widows be considered acceptable. The stakes were high, in a world in which Christians were considered anything but moral and good.

This takes us back to Tabitha and the other widows. They were working, using their skills and resources to put into action the promises of the kingdom, making sure they were doing good and compassionate things. We can imagine Tabitha going from place to place, distributing food and clothing to the needy, telling people about Jesus. Surely someone like Tabitha deserved to live!

In terms of the actual healing, we only get a little glimpse of her perspective. Peter sent everyone else outside, knelt down and prayed, and then said to her, 'Tabitha, rise.' Then she 'opened her eyes, saw Peter and sat up'. He 'gave her his hand and she got to her feet'. Peter called together all the holy ones, including the widows, and showed her to them alive, and the focus then moves to how the news about this miracle led to people's trust in the Lord. Who spread the news? Again, we think of the widows. In this busy port, news would have travelled fast among chains of talkers. People would have wanted to see Tabitha, to know this was true. She could then have given her own testimony.

Later on in Acts, in the 'we-passages', the companion of Paul was clearly with him further up the coast in Caesarea, and the companion travelled to and from Jerusalem. It is quite likely that the story reached the 'I' of this narrative during such a time. Perhaps Tabitha was still living and could tell the story herself; or at least one of the other widows could have done so.

By the writer's choosing to include the story, we don't just learn about a wondrous, life-giving miracle by Peter, but we also learn about a wonderful woman, Tabitha, who provided an example of service. This is not a story about a woman who had a family or a husband, but rather a woman who had a Christian family of brothers and sisters, the 'holy ones and the widows', who loved and cherished her as much as a real family. She was extremely important. In the embrace of such love and faith, and the prayers of Peter, life triumphed.

10

Prisca

The disciple Prisca survives in surprisingly few popular memories. Despite clearly playing second fiddle to his wife in all our biblical texts (Acts 18:2–3, 18–19, 26; Rom. 16:3–4; 1 Cor. 16:19; 2 Tim. 4:19) her husband Aquila was better remembered. A late fourth-century Christian church manual known as the *Apostolic Constitutions* claims that Paul appointed him as one of the first Bishops of Asia Minor. Of Aquila's more illustrious wife, however, nothing is said.

Perhaps the most striking claim surrounding Prisca is the suggestion that she was the author of the New Testament book of Hebrews. This anonymous work, somewhere between a letter and a theological treatise, specifically mentions two women as examples of faith in Chapter 11: Abraham's wife Sarah and Rahab the harlot. Along with the work's compassionate, nurturing tone and interest in childhood (see 2:13–15, 5:11–14 and 12:3–11), this convinced the great German theologian Adolf von Harnack in 1900 that it was written by none other than Prisca. Her name had been suppressed, he suggested, from a sense that a woman should not be given such prominence in the church.

All of this is obviously speculative, and it is extremely difficult to guess at the gender of a work's author on the basis of its contents alone (plenty of male authors display a compassionate tone, and Paul uses the example of Sarah and Hagar in Gal. 4:21–31). Hebrews clearly comes from the pen of a highly educated person who was thoroughly at home with Platonic and Stoic philosophy, and most likely dates from after the destruction of the Jerusalem Temple in 70 CE – all of which seems at odds with what we know of Prisca (as we'll see below). But it is certainly curious that the name of the author of Hebrews was lost, and perhaps even more strange that another wasn't simply supplied. Anonymity or pseudonymity (using someone else's name) is a common strategy for female authors. Whoever actually wrote the text, a connection with the teachings of Prisca – at some level – may not be entirely far-fetched. Harnack might have correctly surmised that she was a woman whose teaching was worth recording.

Both Prisca and Aquila were Paul's 'fellow workers' (Rom. 16:3), meaning that they worked with him on the mission as apostles. An indication of Prisca's standing in the early church is the fact that she is frequently named before her husband. In Acts, Aquila is mentioned first when the couple is introduced (Acts 18:2), but subsequently Prisca is given top billing (18:18, 26). Paul similarly gives Aquila's name first in 1 Corinthians 16:19, but puts Prisca first in Romans 16:3–5 (as does the unknown author of 2 Timothy 4:19). This wouldn't be particularly noteworthy in our own context, but it was highly unusual for an ancient author to name a woman before her husband. It might suggest that Prisca enjoyed higher social standing than her husband, though there is no evidence for this. In the context of our early Christian texts, it's much more likely that Prisca's precedence reflects her higher importance within the new movement. Of the pair, Prisca was the better known and more respected.

Yet, even so, Prisca wasn't immune from efforts to downplay her contribution. An influential fifth-century biblical manuscript known as Codex Bezae (itself part of a wider Western tradition) omits Prisca's name altogether in Acts 18:2 and 18:18, and puts Aquila's name before hers in 18:26 – an alteration that suggests that Aquila was the main teacher of Apollos (on whom, more below).

More generally, Acts downplays the couple's missionary activity in favour of Paul, who is very much the hero of the second half. In Romans 16:4, for example, Paul throws out a tantalisingly brief reference to Prisca and Aquila having 'risked their necks' for his life. We can only guess at what courage Prisca and her husband showed in defence of Paul, but if this incident was known by the author of Acts, it didn't get included in the account.

At other times, all the characters in this drama are subservient to Acts' particular view of early Christian origins. The author of this work is particularly keen to show that the earliest missionaries took the message first to Jews, and only when it met with resistance did they go to pagans. The point is that Jews had the first option on the new faith, and only when they refused it did God offer it to others. Historically, it's certainly likely that Prisca and others went first to their Jewish kinsfolk in each new place. But we may well suspect that the actual picture was much messier than the linear progression of Acts suggests, and that missionaries took the new faith to pagans well before they had completely lost all hope in the synagogue.

It's also worth mentioning that, in Acts, Prisca is always referred to using the diminutive form of her name, Priscilla, or 'little Prisca'. This is analogous to the way we might refer to a Katherine or a Kate as 'Katie' or 'Katykins'. Diminutives like this tend to be more common in Latin than Greek. So Cicero, for example, calls his beloved daughter 'Tulliola' in his personal letters, but by her proper name 'Tullia' in more formal contexts. The use of the diminutive may suggest that the author of Acts had access to traditions that emerged in circles that were on familiar terms with the apostle Prisca, or even knew her.

Refugee from Rome

What do we actually know about this important woman? Our first clue comes from Acts 18:2, where it's noted that her husband Aquila was from Pontus, the northern region of modern Turkey (see map on page 150). Although nothing is said about Prisca's origin, it's likely that she too was originally a Greek-speaking Jew from Pontus. The author of Luke–Acts likes to subvert expectations, showing that characters are not always as stereotypes might lead us to expect – most famously the Good Samaritan, who proves to be a better neighbour than either a priest or a Levite.

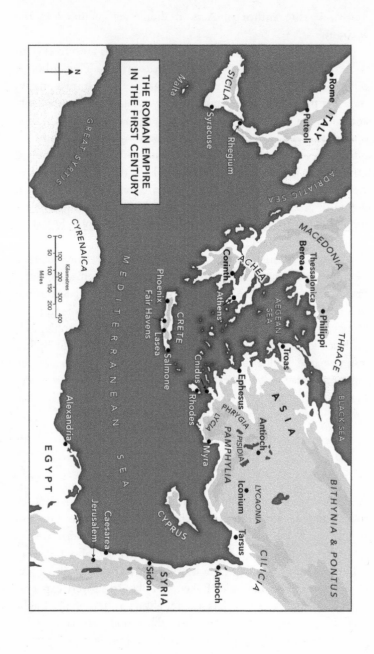

The reason for mentioning the couple's home province is probably because people from Pontus had a reputation for being uneducated barbarians, uncouth and dim-witted people who often found themselves ridiculed for their stupidity. This forms a surprising contrast later on when we read that the couple taught a sophisticated Alexandrian philosopher and intellectual named Apollos. Just as the Good Samaritan overturned audience expectations, here too the reader is surprised that anyone from Pontus should be able to teach such a great and learned man. The reference to Pontus fits this rhetoric, but there is no reason to assume that it's not historically accurate. When we first hear of Prisca, however, she is no longer in Pontus, but has recently been expelled from the capital city of Rome (Acts 18:2).

By the middle of the first century, there was a large and prosperous Jewish population in Rome, settled mainly along the banks of the Tiber and centred on a number of synagogues. Many had come to the city as prisoners of war following Pompey's conquest of Palestine in 63 BCE and had been sold as slaves. A tiny percentage had risen to become Roman citizens, and though many were freed persons, most still belonged to the lowest classes.

Rome was generally tolerant of Jews and other foreign groups. They were allowed to practise their religion in peace, to gather freely to observe the Sabbath, and were exempt from military service. Every now and then, however, there were outbreaks of mistrust and resentment. Jews had been expelled from the city in 19 CE under the Emperor Tiberius. Although the reasons for this are not entirely clear, it may have had something to do with the numbers of Jewish immigrants who were coming into the city and converting Romans away from the traditional cultic practices. Economics may also have played a part: many Jews were poor and depended on the grain dole; by expelling large numbers, Tiberius could save a great deal of money.

The expulsion that Prisca was caught up in took place around thirty years later, in the time of the Emperor Claudius. The exact reasons for the expulsion are far from clear, though the Roman biographer Suetonius claims that Claudius expelled Jews from Rome because of riots at the instigation of someone called

Chrestus. Chrestus was a common slave name (it means 'helpful'), but it is possible that Suetonius got the name wrong and that the riots were actually over 'Christus', that is, Christ. If so, the problem may have been upheavals in certain synagogues caused by missionaries bringing the new faith to the capital city. Acts has it that 'all the Jews' were expelled, but this seems unlikely (and it's not backed up by Suetonius). More probably only the ringleaders were affected, both the Christian missionaries and the synagogue leaders caught up in the fray. As long as the others kept a low profile, it's unlikely that the Roman authorities would have worried too much about them.

Roman citizens couldn't be expelled without trial, so although Prisca and Aquila both had Latin names, it's very unlikely that they were citizens. They may have been from the lower social classes and made their way to Rome in search of work, or perhaps they were freed slaves. The fact that they were caught up in Claudius' expulsion suggests that they were already leaders in the earliest Christian congregations in Rome. How they became believers is anyone's guess. According to Acts 2:9, Jews from Pontus were present at Pentecost – so were Prisca and Aquila in Jerusalem then, and were they among the first to take the new faith to the capital? We can't be sure, but the presence of Christian believers in Rome at such an early date shows just how partial our historical accounts are. So much of the early Christian story has been lost.

By the time we meet them in Acts we have no idea how old they were, or how long they had been part of the Christian community in Rome. It's hard to imagine what it would have been like for Prisca to have been expelled from a city she had made her home. These must have been extremely challenging times: the courage and optimism that she had first brought to her preaching activity had now been met with hostility and division, tensions and all-out riots. The imperial edict that Jews were to be expelled would have seemed like a disaster, ruining all her plans to bring the new faith to her fellow Jews and putting her life, and those of her loved ones, in danger. Many of those caught up in the rioting were presumably too well known to remain in the city: some probably made a quick getaway, spirited away by those willing to put their heads above the parapet; others may have been ferreted out, perhaps handed over by former friends and acquaintances. Several hundreds of people would have been forced to migrate, to suffer the trauma of uprootedness and turned almost overnight into refugees.

Prisca and her husband left Rome by boat and made their way to Corinth, a journey of around five days with a good wind behind them. Travelling by sea was much quicker than by land. Commercial ships transported cargo across the Mediterranean on a daily basis, and would happily take paying passengers as long as they supplied their own food and bedding. We might have romantic ideas of the missionary couple sailing across an idyllic blue Ionian Sea, and perhaps it was like that. But sea travel was not without its dangers from pirates and other marauders, and even experienced sailors were at the mercy of the weather, especially over the harsh winter months (when sea travel was quieter but had not entirely ceased). If Prisca and her husband had needed to leave quickly, they may not have had time to wait for the seas to calm. Roman women did travel by ship, especially with their husbands, though we might imagine that it was not the most comfortable or dignified of journeys. Like everyone else, she doubtless prayed constantly for divine protection.

As Rome and its terrors receded, other anxieties would have come to the fore. Would they be safe in their new city? Would they be made welcome? And how could they continue in their missionary activity?

Corinth

Sometime in late 49 CE, Prisca and Aquila arrived in Corinth, the largest, most prosperous city in Greece. Geographically, the city lay on important trade routes between the Peloponnese and northern Greece, and its two harbours allowed it to maintain good communications with the rest of the Mediterranean. As a Roman colony, the city attracted entrepreneurs from all over the eastern Empire (largely, though not exclusively, drawn from the class of freedmen). The resulting mix was vibrant and cosmopolitan, spanning a broad spectrum of social, cultural and religious backgrounds, presumably making it congenial to people recently arrived from Rome. As the capital of the province of Achaia, the city was a prosperous centre of banking and commerce and attracted large numbers of visitors. From Prisca's point of view, the presence of the largest Greek-speaking Jewish community in Greece must have been a tremendous advantage.

According to Acts, Prisca and Aquila set themselves up as tentmakers, a trade they presumably brought with them. Tentmaking was a particularly portable craft, requiring only a good sharp knife, an awl to make holes and a selection of needles. Besides tents to sleep under (which might have been made of either canvas or leather), tentmakers would have made sun awnings for the homes of wealthy customers, canopies for shops and market stalls, and shelters for boats. Between larger commissions they would have been kept busy with smaller jobs – sandals, belts, harnesses and, of course, repairs to all of the above. There is plenty of ancient evidence of women working as artisans, merchants and traders, especially alongside their husbands. Prisca may have learnt her trade from Aquila, or perhaps from her parents as a girl.

Foreigners tended to live together in ancient cities, so Prisca and Aquila most likely made their way to the Jewish quarter. Trades tended to cluster together too – bakers, millers, barbers, butchers, perfumers, goldsmiths, tailors, glassmakers – and the couple may well have sought out others who shared their trade, perhaps receiving hospitality and a welcome from them. They may even have joined a tentmakers' guild, meeting for social purposes, buying supplies at a discount and plugging themselves into a highly useful network. In time, the couple would have rented a shop that doubled up as a workshop.

Most ancient shops were small, perhaps four metres wide and deep, leading off directly from the street. They would be dark at the back, lit with oil lamps and a brazier for warmth in the winter. At the front, large doors could be thrown open, allowing their wares to spill out into the street under a canopy for passers-by to see what was on offer. In the main body of the shop there would be rolls of linen, canvas and leather. This is where the couple would have worked and taken orders from customers. It would have been hard manual work (especially working with leather), with long hours and only the Sabbath off. At the end of the day, the couple would retreat to a little loft above the shop where they ate and slept.

A great advantage of shop work was that it was the perfect place to meet people. No doubt customers were keen to hear of the troubles in Rome, and the workshop provided the perfect semi-private environment to preach the gospel to a range of patrons. Prisca could easily talk to married women as they decided what to buy, to market traders choosing material for a canopy, or to slaves picking up goods for their masters. Other refugees from the Roman riots might have come along to the workshop, finding comfort in familiar faces and shared stories. Most visitors would have been Jewish customers, but perhaps not all – rent collectors and city taxmen would have called in for their dues, along with tourists and other visitors.

In time, the workshop seems to have formed the nucleus of the Corinthian church, with a 'house church' of maybe ten to fifteen people meeting there regularly. We can perhaps imagine the early believers sitting on the rolls of material as they listened to Prisca and her husband preach the good news and breaking bread together.

Around the spring of 50 CE, Paul of Tarsus arrived in Corinth, fresh from a successful missionary trip to Athens. Sharing the same trade as Prisca and her husband, he stayed with the couple, at least initially, and presumably helped them out in the shop. Their shared faith was no doubt another draw for Paul, enabling him to build on their foundations. Paul would later claim to have 'planted the seed' in Corinth himself (1 Cor. 3:6; see also 2 Cor. 10:14), but – to continue the horticultural analogy – it's likely that Prisca and Aquila had previously tilled the soil. It's all too easy to fall into the trap of reconstructing history as the deeds of great men, particularly in the past when women's activities so often went unnoticed, or they were at best seen as quasi-invisible 'helpers'. Without wanting to detract from Paul's obvious energy and drive, his work in Corinth must have been supported by many whose names have long since perished.

Early Christian meeting places

Jesus told his disciples to use people's homes as a base for reaching a local community (Mark 6:10; Luke 9:4; 10:7). Once the movement spread into the Mediterranean world after Jesus' death, we find early groups of Christ-followers again meeting in homes. Several of these are mentioned in the New Testament: the homes of Prisca and Aquila that we have noted here, Mary the mother of John Mark (Acts 12:12), Lydia (Acts 16:12–15), Nympha (Col. 4:15), Philemon and Apphia (Philem. 1–2), and many more.

The author of Acts gives the impression that homes were the most common place to meet (Acts 1:13), but it's clear that Christian gatherings could take place in a variety of places and settings, from shops, workshops and baths to outdoor spaces and burial grounds. From early on they met on a Sunday (the day of Christ's resurrection), presumably after the day's work was finished, to celebrate the Eucharist and share teaching. In many respects, their gatherings were similar to those of pagan cult societies or voluntary associations (local trade guilds or clubs who met together for shared meals and company in honour of a particular god). Given that the house tended to be the woman's domain, we may wonder whether women might have enjoyed greater leadership responsibilities in domestic settings, particularly when the church met in their own homes (the above list suggests that a surprisingly high number of women were remembered as opening their homes to Christian gatherings).

Paul's practice was to preach in the synagogue, where he was soon joined by his fellow apostles Silas and Timothy. Although Acts is silent on the matter, it's very likely that Prisca and Aquila also shared their new faith with other Jews on the Sabbath. There would have been several synagogues in a city the size of Corinth and it made sense for the earliest missionaries to preach the good news as widely as possible. Prisca and her fellow missionaries were, of course, Jews, and were still regarded as such by the synagogue and themselves.

When tension began to break out – as it had done in Rome – it would not have been primarily for *theological* reasons. There were many different ways of living a Jewish life in this period. The Pharisees and Sadducees, known from the Gospels, had quite striking differences in their legal interpretations yet were generally able to rub along together. Jews were usually tolerant of other Jews, as long as the basics were adhered to (the oneness of God, the place of the Law and the story of Israel). Perhaps what riled the synagogue authorities in Corinth was the zeal of these Christ-following Jews, their sense that they were living in the end of time and their mission to persuade as many people as possible to join them.

Acts 8:5–8 tells of an incident where Paul was asked to leave a synagogue after his preaching led to a heated dispute. He left, but took several members with him, along with a prominent leader named Crispus. At the same time, he seems to have thrown in his lot with a wealthy Roman citizen named Titius Justus. This man was a 'God-fearer,' a pagan who was attracted to Jewish ways and attended the synagogue, but who had stopped short of formal conversion (perhaps because of civic duties that required the worship of pagan gods).

Epigraphic evidence suggests that most God-fearers were women, perhaps reluctant to join a religion not shared by others in their family. A man like Titius Justus would have been an important ally to the Jewish community; he could well have donated to the synagogue and might have been expected to represent Jewish interests in the city more widely, perhaps even to the Roman governor. No doubt his patronage had been highly valuable, and those who remained in the synagogue resented his loss. The Christ-believing Jews who left with Paul, however, gained the use of what was probably a large Roman-style house, with a vestibule open to the street where perhaps thirty or forty believers could congregate at a time. In all probability, this now became their primary meeting place.

Those joining the Christ-followers would have been formally baptised as a sign of their new allegiance. Luke mentions this briefly, but without giving any details. It is possible that it took place in the local public baths (where people of all classes tended to go in the afternoon and where there would be a ready water supply). It's perhaps more likely, though, that baptisms took place at a natural spring. One possibility is that Christians used the famous Peirene Fountain (named after a mythical woman whose son was accidentally killed by Artemis).

If baptisms did happen at busy public places, this strange activity may have begun to attract attention from wider groups of people in the city. Quite probably – as we saw with Mary Magdalene and others in Jesus' circle – it would have been Prisca who baptised women wishing to join the new movement. She would have had easy access to women's quarters and female gatherings, and could have acted as their primary contact and teacher.

The Isthmian Games were celebrated in 51 CE, the second largest games in Greece (only the Olympics were bigger), held every two years in honour of Poseidon. The Games incorporated not only athletic contests, but also competitions in music, oratory and drama. During the Games the city would be full of poets, philosophers, writers and orators – all reciting their works to any who cared to listen. The Games may have led to extra trade from 'pop-up' market stalls, for tents to shelter the overflow crowd and for the tourists who travelled to the city, but it's also likely that Prisca and others took whatever time they could spare to speak to the crowds.

Increasingly, these new converts were coming from all over the Empire, and from a variety of religious backgrounds, not just the Jewish synagogue. While Jews were accustomed to worshipping only one God, however, polytheistic pagans were not. Pagan worship wasn't exclusive, and there was nothing to stop someone revering as many gods as she or he wanted – a new god could be effortlessly absorbed into a rich tapestry of the divine. The requirement to abandon their previous forms of worship must have been a challenge on many levels, not least the break with the gods of the family and the state. To other pagans – those outside the Christian movement – abandoning one's ancestral traditions was both dangerous and offensive. The whole point of religion was to ensure the benevolence of the gods, and deliberately turning one's back on them was inexplicably disloyal and tantamount to atheism.

It's probably for this reason that certain synagogue leaders denounced Paul before the Roman governor, Gallio (who was proconsul of Achaia from 51–52 CE). What worried them was not so much tensions within the synagogues (they could presumably deal with these themselves), but fear that the actions of Paul and his fellow apostles might reflect negatively on the Jewish community as a whole. Jews depended on Roman toleration and acceptance of ways that often struck pagans as odd (the Sabbath rest, for example, or refusal to venerate the city gods). The delicate balance of interests in an ancient pagan city required Jews, in turn, to keep a low profile. So soon after the Roman riots, Jews in other cities would have been particularly careful not to draw attention to themselves. If Paul, Prisca and others were converting pagans, and those pagans were openly rejecting the Roman gods, that would all reflect badly on the Jewish synagogue. By openly denouncing them, the Jewish leaders were effectively distancing themselves from the Christ-following missionaries, showing that these people were no longer part of the Jewish community.

In the end, the plan failed. Gallio refused to be drawn into what he saw as intra-Jewish disputes and dismissed the case (Acts 18:12–17). Yet the hostilities would no doubt remain, especially as increasing numbers of pagans joined the new movement.

Under their founding missionaries, the small Christian community grew and flourished. Their very success, however, caused certain problems. Numbers were soon too great for everyone to meet together (even the homes of the wealthiest members, such as Titius Justus, as we've seen, wouldn't have been able to accommodate more than forty), and as the community found itself spread across various house churches there was an inevitable loss of unity.

At this stage, of course, there were no Gospels, creeds or church manuals. Early Christian 'theology' was not static, and it was the task of the leading missionaries themselves to work out the significance of the cross and precisely what it meant to be a believer in the Roman world. It's no surprise to find questions and concerns presenting themselves almost from the start. To what extent was Christian identity exclusive? Could they maintain contact with earlier cultural and religious allegiances? Could they eat meat that had been sacrificed to idols? What was the place of marriage and children? Could women prophesy? And what about members engaging in immoral behaviour?

Around the autumn of 52 CE, Prisca left for Ephesus, along with Paul and Aquila. Perhaps wealthy members of the church paid for their passage, anxious for them to be able to take the good news elsewhere. Paul kept in contact with the church through letters, though it's clear from 1 Cor. 5:9 (where he mentions an earlier letter) that not all of these letters have survived.

Perhaps Prisca also kept in touch, especially with the women. Like Paul, she might have used a secretary, and she would have found plenty of people who could have taken a letter back with them to Corinth. Did she stay in touch with Chloe perhaps, a prominent Christian woman who led a church in her home (1 Cor. 1:11)? Or Phoebe, a leader of a congregation in the nearby port of Cenchreae (Rom. 16:1–2)? Did Prisca share her views on marriage, morality and female prophecy? And were her thoughts drowned out by the more dominant (and later canonically sanctioned) voice of Paul?

Ephesus

From Corinth, Prisca and her companions sailed across the Aegean Sea to Ephesus, the gateway to Asia – the richest and most populous province in the Roman Empire. Ephesus was the leading city of Asia, home of the governor and provincial government, and a centre of communication and trade. As was the case in Corinth, the city could boast a large and well-integrated Jewish community.

Although Paul arrived in Ephesus with his married companions, he seems to have quickly left them behind and continued on to Jerusalem. The pattern of ministry seems to mirror earlier events in Corinth, with Prisca and Aquila laying the foundation for the Christian community in the city, only to be joined by Paul later. Presumably they repeated what they had done in Corinth, opening a shop and preaching in the synagogues. By the time Paul wrote to the Corinthians, probably midway through 54 CE, Prisca and Aquila sent greetings too, along with their house church (1 Cor. 16:19, 8).

It was in Ephesus that Prisca came across Apollos, a learned and eloquent Jew from Alexandria in Egypt. This man had been baptised with the water-only immersion of John the Baptist (which did not include the imparting of the Spirit) and knew something of the teaching of Jesus, but his knowledge seems to have been incomplete in some way. When Prisca and Aquila heard him speaking in the synagogue, they took him aside and explained things more accurately to him (Acts 18:24–27). He may not have known anything of the development of 'the Way' over the previous few years, and this may have been what the couple needed to tell him. Or maybe they were able to quote passages from the Jewish Scriptures that were fulfilled by Jesus. Perhaps they took him to their home, offered him hospitality and taught him there.

The fact that Prisca's name is in primary position here, of all places, surely suggests that she took the lead in educating Apollos. We've already seen that Acts' readers would have been surprised to find a woman from Pontus teaching a learned Alexandrian. In a Mediterranean honour–shame culture, many men would have refused to be taught by a woman. If Prisca taught Apollos at home, that would have made the whole undertaking less shameful for him, but presumably Prisca was a woman who easily commanded respect. Whether she had any formal education herself is unknown (and seems unlikely), but she was clearly someone who picked things up quickly and could argue and communicate with ease. (We hear of another female teacher in Revelation 2:20 a few decades later, though the author clearly disapproves of her, referring to her as 'Jezebel' after the Old Testament Queen who challenged Elijah.)

Some time later, Apollos decided to go to the province of Achaia, probably to Corinth (we know he ended up there). Acts has it that the *adelphoi* in Ephesus wrote him letters of recommendation (Acts 18:27). This does not necessarily exclude Prisca – Greek, as we've seen, tends to use the masculine plural even when women are included (this is why the NRSV translates it as 'believers' here). Given Prisca's links with the church at Corinth, it would be only natural for her to have contributed to writing the letter for Apollos. And we might wonder whether it was partly her recommendation and teaching that led some in Corinth to prefer Apollos to Paul (see 1 Cor. 1:12; 3:4–7; 4:6).

Back to Rome

When we last hear of Prisca, she had returned to Rome with her husband. With the death of Claudius in Autumn 54 CE, his earlier expulsion of Jews from the city would have lapsed, and so the couple probably felt safe to return and to pick up the pieces of their earlier life. The move may, however, have been more strategic than this. Paul wrote to the church in Rome in the mid- to late-50s CE, and sent greetings to a number of people at the end of the letter (see chapter 12). He mentions Prisca and Aquila first, praising them as fellow workers, and greets the church that met in their home (Rom. 16:3–5).

Given that Paul himself planned to visit Rome soon, what we have here seems to be the familiar pattern of Prisca and Aquila going ahead and assembling a community in the city in preparation for Paul's arrival. Paul presumably expected that his friendship with them would count in his favour with the Roman congregation, and also that they would lend their support to Phoebe as she explained the contents of his lengthy letter. Once again, we have the impression that the influence of Prisca and her husband was significantly greater than the selective history of Acts would suggest. We can only imagine how Prisca welcomed Phoebe and helped her to carry out her mission in an unknown city. After several years of moving from one city to another, Prisca would have fully appreciated the demands of travel and the difficulties of establishing oneself in a new community.

We don't know what became of Prisca and her husband. It would be nice to think of them hosting a church in Rome for many years. More ominously, they may have been caught up in Nero's persecution of Christians in 64 CE. If they were still in the city, it seems unlikely that people of such prominence in the community would have escaped the persecution. If so, they may have eventually died as martyrs for their faith.

Phoebe, Junia and the Women
of the Roman Church

A surprising source of information about early Christian women can be found in the final chapter of Paul's letter to the Romans. Written most probably from Corinth around 55–57 CE, this was Paul's longest letter, containing the fullest and most thought-through account of his theological vision. Unlike the rest of his letters, it was addressed to a church that Paul hadn't yet visited, though he hoped to travel there soon on his way to Spain. It was probably Paul's lack of personal contact with the church that led him to include a list of people he knew in the Roman church in 16:1–16; he clearly expected that they would vouch for him and his message.

As we noted already in the Introduction, the list contains twenty-nine names with the briefest of descriptions. Until recently it tended to be largely ignored by scholars, though in many ways it's a treasure trove of information about one ancient church – a snapshot of people with the names underneath still intact while the faces have long since faded away. What's particularly startling about this list is that just over one-third of the names – eleven of them – belong to women, and it's worth pausing for a moment to reflect on the information that we do have. Some are no more than brief mentions, and we can only guess at their stories: Mary 'who has worked very hard among you' (was she one of the Mary's we have encountered previously in the Gospels and Acts?); Tryphaena and Tryphosa, 'those workers in the Lord' (were they missionaries?); the beloved Persis, who 'has worked hard in the Lord' (was she from Persia, as her name suggests?); the mother of Rufus, 'a mother to me also' (when had she had the opportunity to care for and protect Paul?); Nereus' sister; and of course the women included in the households of Aristobulus, Narcissus, various house churches and 'the saints' generally.

Three women stand out in particular: Phoebe, Prisca and Junia. With the possible exception of Prisca, none of these are household names, and yet we'll see in this chapter that they played authoritative roles at a decisive time in early Christian history. We've already met Prisca (Chapter 10), who had moved back to Rome with her husband Aquila, where they had set up their own house church and were presumably preparing the way for Paul's visit. We'll concentrate in what follows on Phoebe and Junia.

Phoebe – an early Christian leader and interpreter

Phoebe stands at the top of the list and, rather than greet her, Paul commended her to the Roman churches. Clearly, she was a visitor to the city and needed something of an introduction. Paul's short biography, however, has been translated in various ways. Consider Romans 16:1–2 in the New King James Version:

> I commend to you Phoebe our sister, who is a servant of the church in Cenchrea, that you may receive her in the Lord in a manner worthy of the saints, and assist her in whatever business she has need of you; for indeed she has been a helper of many and of myself also.

The impression is of a good, pious woman from the port of Cenchreae (to the east of Corinth), perhaps engaged in menial work, a 'helper', who has been generally useful within the congregations – even lending a hand to Paul himself. It's the typical story of so many women in the church; no wonder few later readers even noticed her. But we get a very different slant from the New Revised Standard Version, which reads:

> I commend to you our sister Phoebe, a deacon of the church at Cenchreae, so that you may welcome her in the Lord as is fitting

for the saints, and help her in whatever she may require from you,
for she has been a benefactor of many and of myself as well.

Now Phoebe is introduced as a 'deacon' – the only woman in the
New Testament to have this title – and a 'benefactor of many',
including Paul. With just a couple of translational changes,
Phoebe is now revealed as a leading woman in the church, a
person of wealth and influence. But even this obscures the full
extent of her impact.

The word translated 'deacon' is *diakonos* in Greek. We've met
this word several times before, particularly as a verb where it is
often used of church ministry. Ordinarily it would mean a servant
(as in the NKJV), but in church contexts it refers to a 'deacon' or
'minister' (and would certainly have been translated in this way if
Phoebe had been a man). What's confusing is the fact that the
countercultural value system of the early church gave menial titles
to what were in effect leadership roles. We can be sure that Phoebe
was a leader of the church in Cenchreae, and presumably a person
of authority and standing.

Even more open to inaccurate translation is the other word
used to describe her, *prostatis*, which is translated as 'helper' in the
NKJV. In its masculine form, this means someone who (quite
literally) stands ahead of anyone else in terms of status; it can be
translated as 'leader', 'ruler' or 'patron'. Any of these leadership
positions might involve acting as a benefactor, but the term itself
implies more than simply bankrolling a local congregation. The
NKJV's 'helper' is woefully inadequate here, and even the NRSV's
'benefactor' doesn't quite capture the prestige in which this
woman was clearly held.

But we can infer more about Phoebe. We've already seen that
Paul was an ardent letter writer; in the first century it was the only
way to keep in touch with other church groups. There was a
system of Roman mail, but it was only for the use of the military
or administrative officials, so when individuals wanted to send
letters they relied on personal couriers, people who were going to
the letter's destination anyway and were willing to take it along
with them. The clear significance of Paul's commendation of

Phoebe is that she was the bearer of the letter. Letter writers often introduced the person who had agreed to carry the missive, and Paul similarly commended Epaphroditus in Philippians 2:25–30.

In order to make the trip to Rome, Phoebe would have needed to cross Corinth from her home in the eastern port of Cenchreae to the western (and more important) port of Lechaeum; she could presumably have met with Paul and picked up the letter on the way. We have no idea what her own business might have been in Rome (it may – or may not – have been church related), but presumably she made the trip by boat, accompanied by others.

The disciples in Rome were asked to help Phoebe in whatever she might require. They were supposed to serve her. She was the one who could ask and receive. She was named first, because Paul wanted to ensure that she was treated with the respect she deserved.

All this is hugely significant. Paul has, of course, often been regarded as a misogynist (George Bernard Shaw dubbed him 'the eternal enemy of woman'*), but much of the negativity in his letters is in fact from the pens of later scribes (see the discussion of the 'insertion' at 1 Corinthians 14:34–35 on p. 180). Paul's letter to Rome was the most important he'd ever write; for him to entrust it to the care of a woman says a great deal about her standing and trustworthiness (and Paul's attitude to women).

Yet even this is not the full story. Given the low literacy rates at the time, it's likely to have been Phoebe who read out the letter to the various Roman congregations, and it would have been Phoebe, too, who explained its meaning, interpreted difficult passages and helped the Roman congregations to understand Paul's thoughts. Phoebe can rightly be seen as the first Pauline interpreter (though we can't know whether she agreed with every passage!).

Straight after commending Phoebe, Paul greets Prisca and Aquila and the church that met in their house. They were old

---

*G. B. Shaw, 'The Monstrous Imposition upon Jesus', reprinted in *The Writings of St. Paul*, ed. Wayne A. Meeks and John T. Fitzgerald (New York, NY: Norton, 2007), p. 417.

friends, of course, and Paul's note that they had 'risked their necks' for his life may cover any number of times that these fellow missionaries had suffered hardship or danger. They knew Paul better than anyone, and it's clear that he would have trusted them with his life – and no doubt his letter. It's significant that the couple are at the top of the list of greetings. We might imagine that Phoebe would have taken the letter to their house church first, expecting a warm welcome both for herself (she no doubt knew the couple from Corinth) and the letter's message.

The situation in Rome was a volatile one. We've already taken note of the riots that led to the expulsion of both synagogue leaders and Christian missionaries in 49 CE (see Chapter 10). Clearly, those who were displaced at that time were now returning to the city (as Prisca and Aquila had already done), but we can imagine that tensions might still have remained, not least within the Christian congregations that had lost their first leaders and were now having to adapt to their return. Paul would never make it to Rome as a free man (his final trip was as a prisoner), and we don't know how his letter went down with the congregations in the divided city. No doubt Phoebe and Prisca did their best to represent his vision to the various house groups.

Junia

Our second woman has had a curious afterlife – largely as a man! Readers with older translations of the Bible will search in vain for 'Junia' in Romans 16, finding only a certain 'Junias' in verse 7. Her story is a good example of unconscious – or conscious! – bias on the part of interpreters, something that has plagued the study of early Christian women.

A fairly literal translation of the relevant verse runs as follows (this is the NRSV):

> Greet Andronicus and Junia, my relatives who were in prison with me; they are prominent among the apostles, and they were in Christ before I was.

The natural way to read this verse is that Paul is referring to a man and woman – Andronicus and Junia. It's the note that they were 'prominent among the apostles' that has caused all the difficulty. Although some suggest that Paul meant that the pair were *highly regarded by* the apostles, the much more natural reading here is that the great missionary refers to both of them – Junia included – as apostles. The earliest interpreters took this in their stride, counting Junia as a prominent female apostle (despite their own rather conventional views on male authority).

By medieval times, however, the reference to a female apostle had become problematic, and another translation began to assert itself. The name of the apostle is in what's known as the accusative case (*Iounian*). It could be translated by the very well-known female name Junia, or – in theory – by the otherwise unknown masculine name Junias. Only accents could show which version was to be preferred, and our earliest Greek texts don't contain any. Despite the fact that Junias is nowhere attested as a male name, medieval translators began to translate the name in this way, suggesting that Paul refers here to a pair of male missionaries – Andronicus and Junias. This dubious reading gained greater traction when it was backed by Martin Luther, who included it in his highly influential German translation, and it was the dominant reading until the 1970s. Since then, feminist interpreters have worked hard to restore Junia to her original gender – and few scholars today would doubt that Paul refers here to a female apostle named Junia.

But what exactly was at stake here? It's clear from Paul's letters that his own status as an apostle was something he had to fight for – not all missionaries were universally acknowledged as apostles. The term 'apostle', as we've seen, refers to one sent out, but much depended on who was doing the sending. The author of Luke (who used the term frequently) reserved it for the disciples of Jesus who were actually commissioned by Christ. Although Paul was clearly the hero in Acts, this author resolutely refused to call him an apostle. Paul, however, used the term rather more widely. So he could refer to Barnabas, Jesus' brothers, Silvanus and Apollos as 'apostles', simply because they were sent out by the earliest churches (see also 1 Corinthians 15:5–7 which mentions 'all the apostles' along with the Twelve). It was also Paul's preferred title for himself, following his commissioning by the risen Lord on the Damascus Road (Paul neatly saw himself as the *last* apostle commissioned by Jesus). But where does all of this leave Junia?

There's reason to believe that Junia's claim to being an apostle would have been rather more generally acknowledged even than Paul's. Andronicus and Junia may have been simply co-workers, but were perhaps more likely to have been a married couple, rather like Prisca and Aquila. Paul describes them as 'relatives', which may mean that they were his kin, but more likely means that they were Jews like him. He also notes quite clearly that they had been 'in Christ' longer than him, which pushes things back quite considerably. Given that Paul joined the new faith within three years or so of the crucifixion, it seems likely that Junia and her husband were Jews from Roman Judaea who had joined the new movement either during Jesus' ministry or very shortly afterwards. We would expect such people to have had a very good knowledge of Jesus and his teaching – either from first-hand experience or from the reports of others who had known him personally. As those who had known Jesus died out, such people would have enjoyed a very high reputation within the churches. No wonder Paul describes them as 'prominent among the apostles'.

There's little else we can say about Junia with any confidence. Her name is Latin, though that doesn't necessarily tell us very much about her (Prisca and Aquila are also Latin names, as we saw). Junia was the name of a prominent Roman family, and it is possible that Junia was a former slave who adopted the name of her erstwhile masters when she was freed. If so, it's hard to see how she became a Christ-follower so quickly (was she in Jerusalem for Passover when she met Jesus or his disciples?).

Another suggestion comes from the prominent New Testament scholar Richard Bauckham. Noting that many Jews chose a similar-sounding Latin name when they moved in non-Jewish circles, Bauckham identifies her with Joanna. The sense we've already established of a very early disciple would certainly fit this identification, and we might imagine that someone of Joanna's background and status would be in a good position to play a leading role in the founding and growth of the Roman community. We would then be able to plot Joanna's history from the upper echelons of Tiberias to the roads of Galilee and Judaea, and on to Rome. The difficulty, of course, lies in the names of the 'husbands' (if this is in fact what they are). Without more solid links, the identification can only be an intriguing possibility.

At all events, Paul lavishes praise on Andronicus and Junia. It's clear that, along with Prisca and Aquila, Epaenetus and Mary, they were leaders of the Roman community and people whose good opinion he wanted to encourage. They aren't specifically said to have led a house church, so perhaps they had a broader remit – promoting unity within the various churches, or missionary outreach. Paul knew them already, but wanted to be sure that they would root for him and support his proposed visit. All three of them had something further in common: they had all spent time in prison for their faith.

'In prison with me'

Unlike today, there was little sense in the ancient world of prison being a place of correction or even formal punishment. Most commonly, accused prisoners were put in prison until their case was heard, at which point they would be sentenced to an appropriate punishment – execution, for example, or hard labour (though labourers might be housed in a secure compound much like a prison, sometimes after being blinded to stop them escaping). Debtors might be put in prison, often put to forced labour until the debt was paid (see Matt. 18:28–30; Luke 12:58–59).

John the Baptist was jailed by Herod Antipas rather than executed straight away (presumably Antipas wanted to avoid the public outcry that would follow John's death). And prisons feature twice in Acts: first when the High Priest put the apostles in the public prison (though they were released by an angel, Acts 5:17–25), and a second time when Paul and Silas were imprisoned in

Philippi (this time set free by an earthquake, Acts 16:23–27). In the latter case, the prisoners were flogged first, and then held in the central (most secure) area with their feet in stocks.

Conditions in Roman jails depended on status. For non-citizens, things would have been indescribably harsh. The prison itself might have been a purpose-built dungeon, but was more likely to have been a storeroom, a cave or a pit. Prisoners might have been stripped and flogged, and left to rot in cold, cramped cells, with legs and perhaps arms in shackles, and no toilet facilities. We can only imagine the mental toll of the darkness, or the stench of rotting flesh as wounds became infected. Women would be thrown into jail alongside men, and sexual violence and abuse was common, from either the guards or fellow prisoners. Prison food was poor, and many would no doubt have starved to death.

Prisoners of higher status had better conditions. The nobility might have expected to be detained in the homes of other members of the elite, or even to be held under guard in their own homes or country estates. Paul spent a great deal of time detained and was able to write and send letters, despite his captivity. As a Roman citizen he was placed under house arrest for two years in Rome (after having been held for two years in Caesarea before that). He was able to receive visitors, who were able to provide him with clothes, better food and company.

It's impossible to know when Andronicus and Junia were imprisoned with Paul (though it must have been before his final incarceration). Paul's status would have protected him against the very worst conditions, and if Junia was a freed slave (and so now a citizen) – or even to be identified with Joanna – then that would also have protected her against the very worst conditions. The lack of liberty, though, must have been hard to bear. It's possible that the couple had voluntarily shared his captivity, as other close friends did, such as Epaphroditus (Phil. 2:25-28) and perhaps Aristarchus (Col. 4:10). But it's perhaps more likely that they were prisoners alongside Paul. Were the couple arrested at the same time as Paul, perhaps for disturbing the peace with their preaching? Or were they all handed over to magistrates, as we saw in Corinth? All in all, Paul's brief mention provides us with a tantalising glimpse of an important yet otherwise unknown woman disciple.

The final chapter of Paul's letter to the Romans, then, provides intriguing clues to a number of prominent women in the church of the 50s CE. We see them leading churches, carrying letters and explaining their contents, spreading the Word and suffering imprisonment for their efforts. If only more of their story had survived, the history of the church and the place of women within it might have been very different indeed.

Did Paul really say that women would be 'saved through childbearing' (1 Timothy 2:15)?

1 Timothy, along with 2 Timothy and Titus, form a group of letters known as the pastoral epistles. Although they claim to have come from Paul, the majority of scholars argue that they are 'pseudonymous', or written by someone else in Paul's name. Most likely, the letters come from the early second century; they reflect a much more developed church order than the genuine letters of Paul, and seem to respond to a very different cultural context.

The author was concerned with the way the church looked to outsiders and urged believers to adhere to what he saw as 'natural' age and gender divisions (i.e., older men were to be in charge). There was clearly a problem with women and their activities in the congregations to which the letters were directed, and the author used strong language to keep them in check. The church, he argued, was to be modelled on the (patriarchal) family of God, with the bishop acting as the head. Other members of the group were required to subordinate themselves to him. And just as women, children and slaves were to be submissive within the household, so they should be within the Christian community.

Our author draws on typical female stereotypes – women were gossips (1 Tim. 5:13) and easily duped (2 Tim. 3:6). Women (or wives, it's the same word) were told to learn quietly and submissively and not to have authority over men/their husbands (1 Tim. 2:10–14).

Justification for all of this came from the account of creation in Genesis 1–3, where Adam came first and wasn't deceived (though this is clearly a rather strange reading of the text!). Women would be saved, he reassured them, through or during childbearing, 'provided they continue in faith and love and holiness, with modesty' – that is, by knowing their proper place as submissive wives and mothers.

'Saved through/during childbearing' can't mean that childbearing was the only way to salvation for women, so this statement has led to alternative interpretations and translations. It might even have been a way of reassuring women that they would be protected in childbearing (if they behaved correctly!), and that they should not seek to avoid motherhood like the celibate widows and virgins.

Presumably the author of the pastoral epistles believed he was writing in the spirit of Paul, but his views were a long way from those of the genuine apostle. Quite apart from Paul's obvious delight in his female co-workers and enthusiasm for their activities, when he mentioned Eve's deception, he saw it as relating to humans generally, not women alone (2 Cor. 11:3). And the great missionary advocated celibacy, not childbirth and family life – for men and women (1 Cor. 7) – so that they were able to spread the word. Of course, we don't know how Paul would have responded to the changed circumstances of the early second century, but it is hard to see much similarity between his views and those of the author of 1 Timothy.

Epilogue

Cerula of Naples

Before the Battle of Milvian Bridge in 312 CE, the Emperor Constantine claimed to have seen a cross in the sky, accompanied by a voice saying, 'In this sign, conquer.' Constantine's conversion to Christianity seems to have been genuine enough, though the victory of his troops with a cross now emblazoned on their shields had the added benefit of uniting his previously divided army behind one deity.

Remains of colossal marble sculpture of Constantine (c.312-315), with Helen and Joan, Capitoline Museum, Rome

The sign Constantine used was actually a mixture of the cross and the first letters of the word 'Christ' in Greek (the language of most of his soldiers) – *chi* (X, sometimes on its side) and *rho* (P) – and is known as the *chi-rho* monogram or 'staurogram'. Unsurprisingly, perhaps, the type of Christianity that Constantine embraced was the strongly militant faith that had made great headway among the Roman army, with its promotion of courage and resilience, and its championing of the robust fortitude of martyrs in the recent bloody persecutions. All of this was a long way from Jesus' commands to 'turn the other cheek' and to love one's enemies.

One of the most striking things about Christianity through to the early fourth century was its diversity, with different groups in different contexts living out their faith in a variety of ways. Christian diversity, however, was not a good thing for the Emperor, and when he took charge of the Church he made it his mission to stamp out variants. Constantine presided over a council in Nicaea in 325 designed to systematise the churches in line with the type of Christianity that the army (and he) followed. It will come as no surprise to hear that this was not particularly women friendly. Leadership roles were now exclusively the preserve of men; other rules and regulations, such as divorce laws, favoured men; and women's earlier roles were diminished or forgotten.

We can see clear evidence of the belittling of Jesus' women disciples in the art of the fourth century. In Christian art of the third and early fourth century, women are represented without veils, but this changes quite noticeably so that, by the fifth century,

The Jonah Sarcophagus (late third century)

women are generally veiled and seen to exhibit a high standard of modesty. Those bold, spirited women that we've seen on every page of this book were now cast as demure matrons and virgins, if they were remembered at all.

Not only that, but they can be reduced in size in relation to Jesus and his male disciples, as art historian Ally Kateusz has shown. While in the earliest versions of the raising of Lazarus scene, Martha and Mary are around the same size as Jesus and the male disciples (see page 178), they become progressively smaller with the passing of the fourth century, until the two sisters are represented as one tiny crouching, veiled figure (and often blended with the blood-flow woman), no larger than a small animal (see below). The iconography depicts a clear movement in which women who were originally central to the scene are sidelined, and moved to the periphery, or edited out entirely.

Sarcophagus (late fourth century)

What we have by the fourth century, then, is a combination of the patriarchal impulse within ancient society and the need to minimise women's involvement in the face of outside criticism that we've seen many times already, with the promotion of a decidedly masculine form of Christianity that actively curtailed women's activities and leadership. The central message of servant-hood and *diakonia*, which resonated so well with women's activities, was eclipsed by a framework that promoted images of triumph and imperialism. Successive church councils curbed women's leadership, as baptisers, as prophets, as having any 'ordained' roles as deacons, presbyters (priests) or overseers (bishops). The order of widows was discontinued.

As a result of Constantine's measures, books not approved of by imperial standards (like the *Gospel of Mary*) were burnt. Heretics were excommunicated. And the whole library of Antioch was burnt by order of Emperor Jovian in 364 CE. This was the time in which some of our earliest and most important manuscripts of the New Testament were commissioned, and copied into beautiful volumes by expert scribes. Some of the editorial decisions made by these highly trained scribes have a bearing on the place of women. We'll consider just two examples, both from Codex Vaticanus, a beautiful vellum manuscript containing most of the Bible and housed in the Vatican Library. Largely because of its age, Vaticanus is one of the most important witnesses to the Greek versions of the New Testament, and hence to our own (translated) English versions. Decisions made by whoever copied out this version, then, have had a tremendous significance over the centuries.

The first example is the little passage in 1 Corinthians 14:34–35 that tells wives to keep silent in the churches. The passage doesn't fit the context and reads a lot like something that has been added later on, as if a marginal note has been included into the main text, presumably to bring the teaching of Paul into line with practice in the author's own day. The verses are found in a variety of different places in other manuscripts, which is often a sign that a later passage has been added. Removing it creates a much better flow to Paul's argument. The apostle acknowledges that women are welcome to prophesy in church in 11:2–16 (albeit with their heads covered); why would he change his mind and command women not to speak just a couple of chapters later? The curious thing about Vaticanus is that the scribe inserted little marginal signs around the passage to indicate that he knew that some manuscripts didn't have the verses and that in all probability they were additions, as biblical scholar Philip Payne has importantly shown. Nevertheless, the scribe still included it – with disastrous consequences for all the women who have been silenced in churches because of this passage.

Our second passage is the story of the woman caught in adultery (John 7:53–8:11), and here it is a sin of omission. This particular story (in which only the woman seems to have been caught *in flagrante*) is one of the most curious in the whole New Testament manuscript tradition. Sometimes early manuscripts include it and sometimes not; it even turns up at times in Luke, rather than John. There are also more variant readings of particular words in this short section than anywhere else in the Gospels. Many scholars think that the instability of the story means that it was not original to John, and so there would be some warrant in omitting it. Still, it is one of the earliest stories about Jesus that we have. Papias of Hierapolis (*c.* 110 CE), who didn't otherwise seem to know the Gospel of John, seems to have known a version. It turns up in the Didascalia Apostolorum. And in the fourth century, Eusebius knew the story, though he associated it with the Gospel of the Hebrews (Eusebius, *Church History* 3:39:16).

The memory of this woman, and Jesus' reaction to her, is found in both East and West in manuscripts of the Gospels and beyond. So what did the copyist of Vaticanus do with this ancient passage, which he knew to be textually insecure? He omitted it completely (and again added marks to tell us this). The reason why he chose not to reproduce it might be found in fourth-century male anxiety. Ambrose, Bishop of Milan, worried that it looked like Jesus had an adulteress presented to him and dismissed her without condemnation (*A Second Defence of David* 1:1,3). Augustine said that certain men 'removed the Lord's act of forgiveness towards the adulterous woman' from the manuscripts, 'fearing in case their wives should be granted impunity in sinning' (*Adulterous Marriages* 2:7). Male interests clearly superseded those of women.

Together, these examples show two passages that were known to be textually insecure, yet our Vaticanus copyist decided to keep in the verses that silenced women but to leave out the story of a woman who was forgiven by Jesus. We could add many more examples to these two. But if a passage like the adulterous woman could be omitted simply to ease male insecurities, what else has been cut out, or burnt, without a trace?

Yet this is not the full story. Despite the dominant discourse that would marginalise women at that time, fragments of texts, inscriptions, art and archaeology allow us to catch fleeting glimpses of women still exercising leadership roles through to the sixth and seventh centuries. Inscriptions show women still acting as presbyters and deacons, widows and virgins. Clearly, the memories of those first-century Christian sisters refused to be eradicated, and provided role models and inspiration for later generations of women. However much scribal activities and male interpretation sought to subdue them, the legacies of those pioneering women refused to be completely overlooked. One ancient portrait brings this sharply into focus.

Cerula of Naples (late fifth century)

In the vast catacombs of Naples, many images adorn the walls of recesses that once contained the bones of countless Christians. Two portraits from the fifth and sixth centuries are particularly intriguing. They are of two women, named Cerula (or Cervia) and Bitalia. Both are free from jewellery and veiled, with only their upper bodies showing. Both are in a praying position with their arms raised, and with the *chi-rho* monogram of Christ's victory (with Alpha and Omega) above their heads. They both wear a short *pallium* or cloak over their shoulders, which seems to have been liturgical clothing in this period. Cerula's pallium is finely represented, with a design containing numerous figures (many praying like her) and medallions with crosses inside. Most striking of all, however, is that they are shown with open books containing the four Gospels and emitting tongues of fire (probably to indicate the Spirit, which comes from the texts). Cerula is grey-haired, and perhaps a little older than Bitalia; the figures of Peter and Paul stand on either side of her in separate panels.

What are we to make of these images? It wasn't uncommon at the time to represent female literacy with a scroll, and it could be argued that the inclusion of the fourfold Gospel codex might indicate female teachers or deacons. Depictions of the Gospels, however, are extremely rare, and these – along with the liturgical garments – suggest women of much higher status with teaching authority. Art historian Ally Kateusz has long worked on interpreting the representations of women in early Christian art, and argues that these women weren't simply prominent members of their churches but that they functioned quite specifically as *bishops*. Her arguments gain weight from the fact that certain Christian authorities were still trying to stamp out women's leadership in and around Naples. Pope Gelasius (in 495 CE) wrote to the bishops in the area that he had heard that 'women are encouraged to serve at the sacred altars, and that all tasks entrusted to the service of men are performed by a sex for which these [tasks] are not appropriate' (*Letters of the Roman Popes* 14). Did Cerula and Bitalia represent such dangerous women, whose leadership needed to be curtailed? Their congregations clearly saw things differently, and greatly honoured them in their burials.

The story of the suppression of women in the Church is a sorry tale that still has repercussions today. Women have been silenced, marginalised, refused entry to theological discussion and blamed for it. As we have seen throughout this book, however, there is a wealth of evidence that tells us that in the earliest period of Christianity women were highly active as disciples and teachers, prophets, missionaries and midwives of the faith. Texts could later be edited or forgotten, and memorials obliterated, but the fact is that the story of Jesus began with a woman who gave birth to him and ended with a woman who witnessed him alive after his death. Jesus was not one to follow social convention, and openly challenged social norms and regional authorities. Women disciples of Jesus were a vital part of his movement, and women spearheaded the growth of the mission in the decades that followed.

Yet women were a liability as the faith spread around the world, at a time when any groups led by women could be ridiculed by (male) opponents. Stories about women in the Gospels and the letters of Paul could make certain men feel uncomfortable and leave the movement open to attack. Three centuries after Jesus, Christianity would be remade to sit comfortably with Roman imperial rule, as the religion of the rich and mighty, at home in the military. Perhaps the first step to unmaking some of the changes is by the power of memory. For this we need not only evidence, but also a firm grasp of the ancient context, and a good dose of informed imagination.

We hope we have set the women disciples of Jesus in their rightful place, close to Jesus in his mission in Galilee, and active in establishing, serving and leading Christian communities as the faith spread around the Mediterranean and the wider ancient world.

The question is: once these women are truly remembered, where will we go from here?

Thanks

Just a final note of thanks to say we are extremely grateful to Jean-Claude Bragard and Anna Cox from Minerva Media, our wonderful allies who made the documentary *Jesus' Female Disciples: The New Evidence* (2018) the great success it was. Their determination, creativity and passion fuelled us every step of the way. Thank you also to Ian Salvage and Jason Lord-Castle, on camera, and Alan Hill, our sound recordist. Thanks, too, to the scholars we interviewed for the programme – Tal Ilan, Philip Payne, and Ally Kateusz – each of you stimulated our thinking and added so much depth to the story.

Thank you to Elizabeth Foy, Manager at St Paul's Cathedral, for inviting us to share our ideas with a huge audience and for putting us in touch with Katherine Venn of Hodder Faith. Katherine has been completely committed to the project from the start, and we couldn't have hoped for a better editor or production team.

We thank as always our husbands and children for their encouragement, humour, love and general delightfulness.

Suggestions for Further Reading

Jesus

Bond, Helen, *Jesus: A Very Brief History* (London: SPCK, 2017).

Bond, Helen, *The Historical Jesus: A Guide for the Perplexed* (London: T&T Clark, 2012).

Donne, Anthony Le, *Historical Jesus: What Can We Know and How Can We Know It?* (Grand Rapids: Eerdmans, 2011).

Fredriksen, Paula, *Jesus of Nazareth, King of the Jews: A Jewish Life and the Emergence of Christianity* (New York: Vintage Books, 1999).

Levine, Amy-Jill, Dale C. Allison and John Dominic Crossan (eds.), *The Historical Jesus in Context*, Princeton Readings in Religions (Princeton, NJ: Princeton University Press, 2006).

McGrath, James, *What Jesus Learned from Women* (Eugene: Cascade, 2021).

Sanders, E. P., *The Historical Figure of Jesus* (New York: Penguin Books, 1993).

Vermes, Geza, *Jesus the Jew: A Historian's Reading of the Gospels* (Philadelphia: Fortress Press, 1981).

Women in the world of Jesus

Brooten, Bernadette J., *Women Leaders in the Ancient Synagogue: Inscriptional Evidence and Background Issues* (Chico: Scholars Press, 1982).

Ilan, Tal, *Jewish Women in Greco-Roman Palestine: An Inquiry into Image and Status* (Texte und Studien zum Antiken Judentum 44, Tübingen: J. C. B. Mohr, 1995).

Kraemer, Ross S. and D'Angelo, Mary Rose (eds.), *Women and Christian Origins* (New York and Oxford: Oxford University Press, 1999).

Parks, Sara, Shayna Sheinfeld and Meredith J. C. Warren, *Jewish and Christian Women in the Ancient Mediterranean* (London: Routledge, 2021).

Taylor, Joan E., *Jewish Women Philosophers of First-Century Alexandria: Philo's 'Therapeutae' Reconsidered* (Oxford: Oxford University Press, 2003).

Female disciples of Jesus (and their presentation in the Gospels)

Bauckham, Richard, *Gospel Women: Studies of the Named Women in the Gospels* (London: T&T Clark, 2002).

Conway, Colleen M., *Men and Women in the Fourth Gospel: Gender and Johannine Characterization* (Atlanta: Society of Biblical Literature, 1999).

D'Angelo, Mary Rose, '(Re) Presentations of Women in the Gospels: John and Mark', in Ross Shepard Kraemer and Mary Rose D'Angelo (eds.) *Women and Christian Origins* (Oxford: Oxford University Press, 1999), pp. 129–49.

D'Angelo, Mary Rose, 'Women Partners in the New Testament,' *Journal of Feminist Studies in Religion* 6/1 (Spring, 1990), pp. 65–86.

Fehribach, Adeline, *The Women in the Life of the Bridegroom: A Feminist Historical–Literary Analysis of the Female Characters in the Fourth Gospel* (Collegeville, MN: Liturgical Press, 1998).

Fiorenza, Elisabeth Schüssler, *In Memory of Her* (London: SCM, [1983, 1990] 2009).

Levine, Amy-Jill with Maria Mayo Robbins (eds.), *A Feminist Companion to the New Testament Apocrypha* (Cleveland: Pilgrim, 2006).

Seim, Turid Karlsen, *The Double Message: Patterns of Gender in Luke and Acts* (Nashville: Abingdon, 1994).

Taylor, Joan E., 'Two by Two: The Ark-etypal Language of Mark's Apostolic Pairings', in Joan E. Taylor (ed.), *The Body in Biblical, Christian and Jewish Texts* (London: T&T Clark, 2014), pp. 58–82.

Taylor, Joan E., 'Paul's Significant Other in the "We" Passages', in Craig A. Evans and Aaron W. White (eds.) *Who Created Christianity? Fresh Approaches to the Relationship between Paul and Jesus* (Grand Rapids: Hendrickson, 2020), pp. 125–56.

Mary Magdalene

de Boer, Esther A., *Mary Magdalene: Beyond the Myth*, translated by John Bowden (Harrisburg: Trinity Press International, 1997).

de Boer, Esther A. *The Gospel of Mary: Beyond a Gnostic and a Biblical Mary Magdalene* (JSNTS 60, London and New York: T&T Clark, 2004).

Brock, Ann Graham, *Mary Magdalene, the First Apostle. The Struggle for Authority* (Harvard Theological Studies 51, Cambridge, Mass.: Harvard University Press, 2003).

Griffith-Jones, Robin, *Mary Magdalene: The Woman Jesus Loved* (Norwich: Canterbury Press, 1998).

Haskins, Susan, *Mary Magdalen: Myth and Metaphor* (New York: Riverhead, 1993).

King, Karen, *The Gospel of Mary of Magdala: Jesus and the First Women Apostle* (Oregon: Polebridge Press, 2003).

Marjanen, Antti, *The Woman Jesus Loved: Mary Magdalene in the Nag Hammadi Library and Related Documents* (Leiden: Brill, 1996).

Schaberg, Jane, *The Resurrection of Mary Magdalene* (London: Continuum, 2002).

Schrader, Elizabeth and Taylor, Joan E., 'The Meaning of "Magdalene"', *Journal of Biblical Literature* 140 (2021), pp. 751–73

Taylor, Joan E., 'Missing Magdala and the Name of Mary "Magdalene"', *Palestine Exploration Quarterly* 146 (2014), pp. 205–22.

Taylor, Joan E., 'What Did Mary Magdalene Look Like? Images from the West, the East, Dura and Judaea', in Alicia Batten, Sarah Bloesch and Meredith Minister (eds.), *Dress in Mediterranean Antiquity: Greeks, Romans, Jews, Christians* (London: T&T Clark, 2021), pp. 257–78.

Joanna, Susanna and Salome

Bauckham, Richard, 'Salome the Sister of Jesus, Salome the Disciple of Jesus, and the Secret Gospel of Mark', *Novum Testamentum* 33 (1991), pp. 245–75.

Mary and Martha

Ernst, Allie, *Martha from the Margins: The Authority of Martha in Early Christian Tradition* (Leiden: Brill, 2009).

Reinhartz, Adele, 'From Narrative to History: The Resurrection of Mary and Martha', in Amy-Jill Levine (ed.), *Women Like This: New Perspectives on Jewish Women in the Greco-Roman World* (Atlanta: Scholars Press, 1991).

Taylor, Joan E., 'The Bethany Cave: A Jewish-Christian Cult Site?' *Revue Biblique* 97 (1990), pp. 453–65.

Yamaguchi, Satoko, *Mary and Martha: Women in the World of Jesus* (Maryknoll, NY: Orbis, 2002).

The woman with the flow of blood

Fonrobert, Charlotte, 'The Woman with a Blood-Flow (Mark 5:24–34) Revisited: Menstrual Polemics in Christian Feminist Hermeneutics' in Craig A. Evans and James A. Sanders (eds.), *Early Christian Interpretation of the Scriptures of Israel: Investigation and Proposals* (JTNTSup 148; Stanford: Standford University Press, 1997), pp. 121–41.

Schiffman, Larry, 'Matthew 9:20–22: "And Behold, a Woman Who Had Suffered from a Hemmorhage" – The Bleeding Woman in Matthew, Mark, and Luke: Perspectives from Qumran and Rabbinic Literature', in R. Steven Notley and Jeffrey P. Garcia (eds.) *The Gospels in First Century Judaea* (Leiden: Brill, 2016), pp. 5–19.

Mary the mother of Jesus

Kateusz, Ally, *Mary and Early Christian Women: Hidden Leadership* (New York: Palgrave Macmillan, 2019).

Kearns, Cleo McNelly, *The Virgin Mary, Monotheism, and Sacrifice* (Cambridge: CUP, 2008).

Shoemaker, Stephen J., *Mary in Early Christian Faith and Devotion* (New Haven: Yale, 2016).

Phoebe, Junia and Prisca

Epp, Eldon J., *Junia: The First Woman Apostle* (Minneapolis: Fortress, 2005).

Gooder, Paula, *Phoebe: A Story* (London: Hodder and Stoughton, 2018).

Kearsley, Rosalinde A., 'Women in Public Life in the Roman East: Iunia Theodora, Claudia Metrodora and Phoebe Benefactress of Paul', *Tyndale Bulletin* 50 (1999), pp. 189–211.

Seabourne, Che R., 'New Directions in Redaction Criticism and Women', *Theology* 119 (2016), pp. 335–41.

Whelan, Caroline., 'Amica Pauli: The Role of Phoebe', *JSNT* 49 (1993), pp. 67–85.

Yii-Jan, Lin, 'Junia: An Apostle before Paul', *Journal of Biblical Literature* 139 (2020), pp. 191–209.

Women in the early church

Clark, Elizabeth A., *Women in the Early Church* (Minnesota: Liturgical Press, 1983).

Cohick, Lynn H., *Women in the World of the Earliest Christians: Illuminating Ancient Ways of Life* (Grand Rapids: Baker Academic, 2009).

Cooper, Kate, *Band of Angels: The Forgotten World of Early Christian Women* (New York: Atlantic Books, 2013).

Hylen, Susan E. 'Women διάκονοι and Gendered Norms of Leadership, *Journal of Biblical Literature* 138 (2019), pp. 687–702.

Kateusz, Ally and Confalonieri, Luca Badini, 'Women Church Leaders in and around Fifth-century Rome,' in Joan E. Taylor and Ilaria L. E. Ramelli (eds.), *Patterns of Women's Leadership in Early Christianity* (Oxford: Oxford University Press, 2021), pp. 228–60.

Kroeger, Catharine. 'Bitalia, The Ancient Woman Priest', *Priscilla Papers* 7, 11–12.

MacDonald, Margaret, *Early Christian Women and Pagan Opinion: The Power of the Hysterical Woman* (Cambridge: Cambridge University Press, 1996).

Madigan, Kevin and Osiek, Carolyn, *Ordained Women in the Early Church: A Documentary History* (Baltimore, MD: Johns Hopkins University Press, 2005).

Miller, Patricia Cox (ed.), *Women in Early Christianity: Translations from Greek Texts* (Washington, D.C.: The Catholic University of America Press, 2005).

Osiek, Carolyn, Margaret Y. MacDonald and Janet H. Tulloch, *A Women's Place: House Churches in Earliest Christianity* (Minneapolis: Fortress, 2006).

Payne, Philip B. 'Vaticanus Distigme-Obelos Symbols Marking Added Text, Including 1 Corinthians 14.34–5,' *New Testament Studies* 63 (2017), 604–25

Taylor, Joan E. and Ilaria L. E. Ramelli (eds.), *Patterns of Women's Leadership in Early Christianity* (Oxford: Oxford University Press, 2021).

Online:

Kateusz, Ally, 'Disappearing Women at the Raising of Lazarus', http://allykateusz.com/art-as-text-powerpoints/disappearing-women-at-the-raising-of-lazarus/

'Cerula and Bitalia – Women Bishops?', Wijngaards Institute for Catholic Research, http://www.womendeacons.org/cerula-and-bitalia/

Image Credits

Page ix: Joan and Helen © Anna Cox, Minerva Media.

Page 1: *The Last Supper* by Leonardo da Vinci © Mauro Ranzani/ Bridgeman Images.

Page 69: *The Holy Women at the Sepulchre*. Private Collection © Laura James. All Rights Reserved.

Page 75: The blood-flow woman with Jesus, Catacombs of Marcellinus and Peter, Rome. History and Art Collection/Alamy Stock Photo.

Page 95: *Christ in the House of Martha and Mary* by Diego Velasquez. National Gallery London, UK/Bridgeman Images.

Page 123: Tikhvin Icon of the Theotokos and Infant Jesus, St Issac's Cathedral, St Peterburg. Godong/Alamy Stock Photo.

Images on pages ix, 29, 177, 178, 179, 182 © Joan Taylor.

Index